This math workbook
belongs to

____

Table of Contents

Use color pencils or crayons to color the objects.

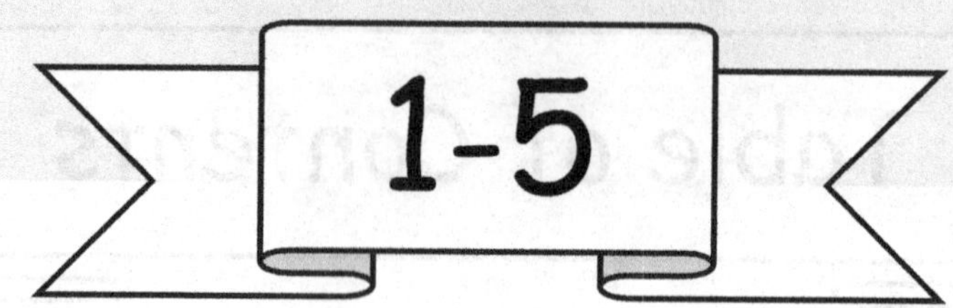

1

2

3

4

5

5

1
One

2
Two

3
Three

4
Four

5
Five

Tracing & Writing 1-5

1 1 One

Tracing & Writing 1-5

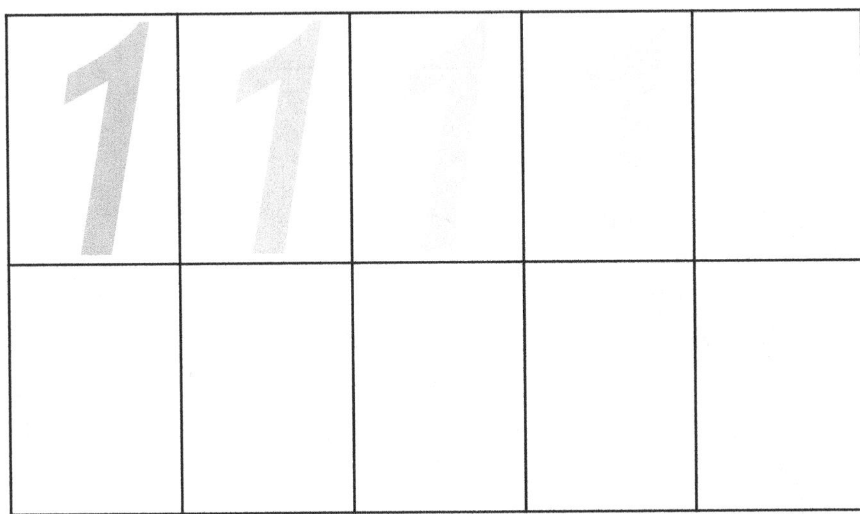

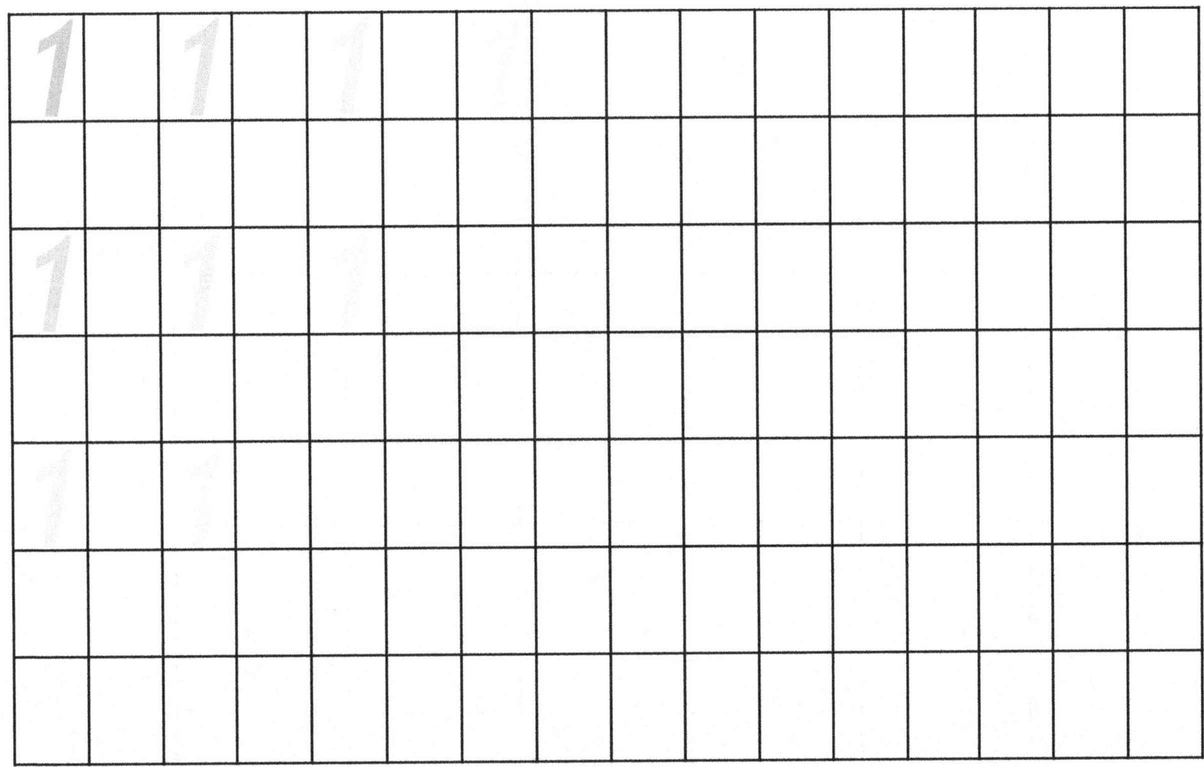

Tracing & Writing 1-5

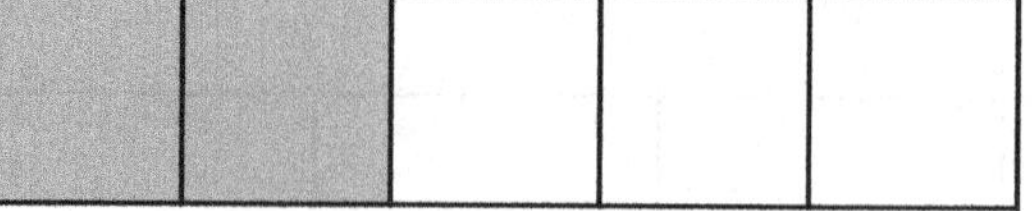

2 2 Two

Tracing & Writing 1-5

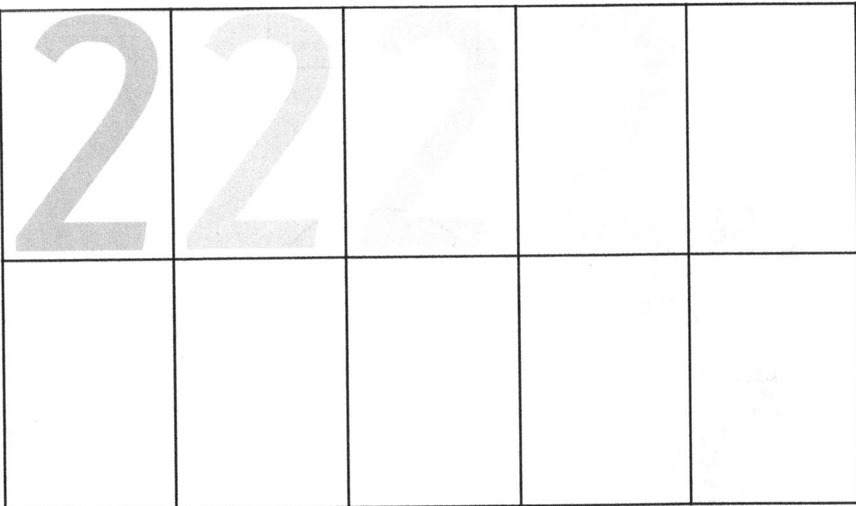

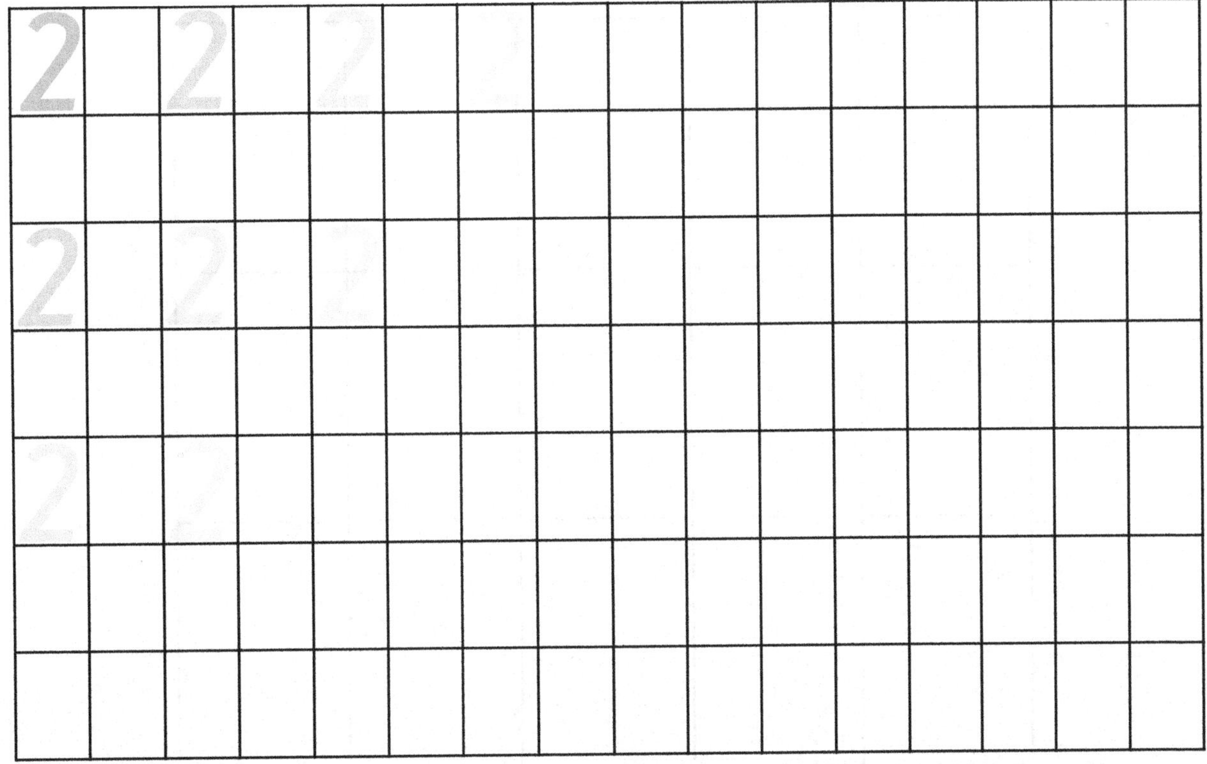

Three

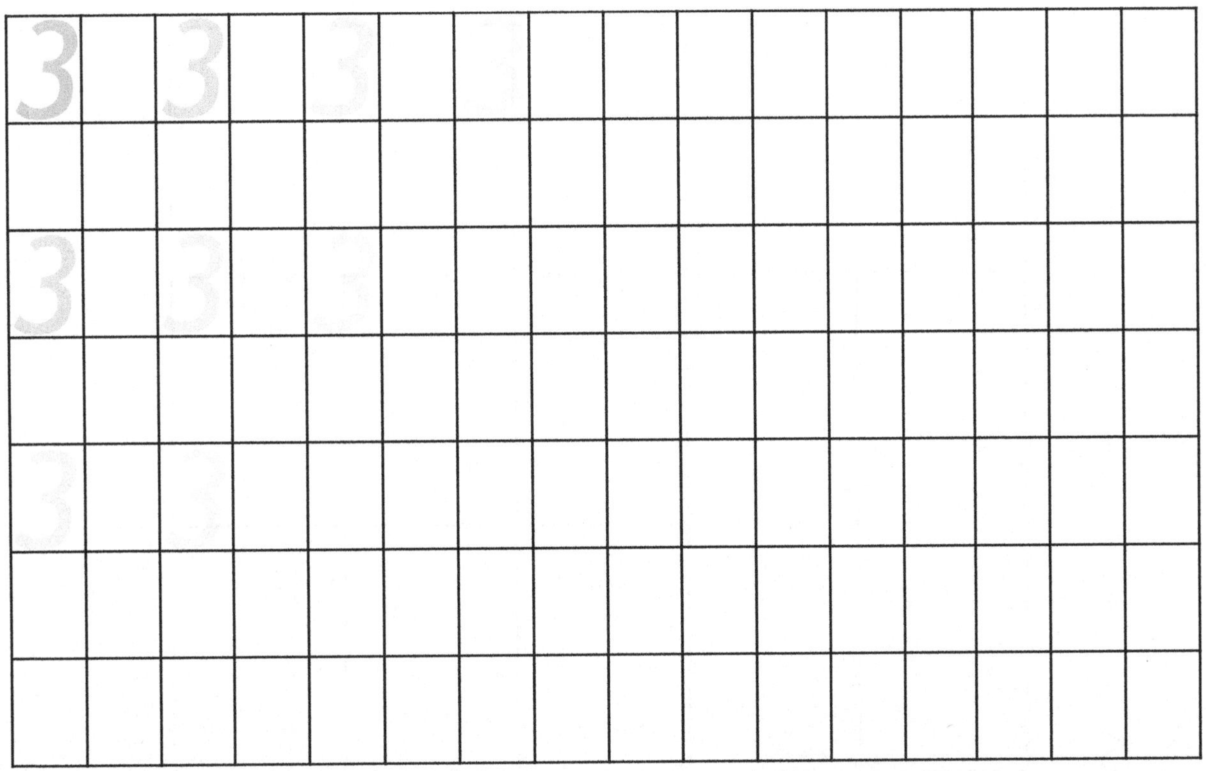

Four

13

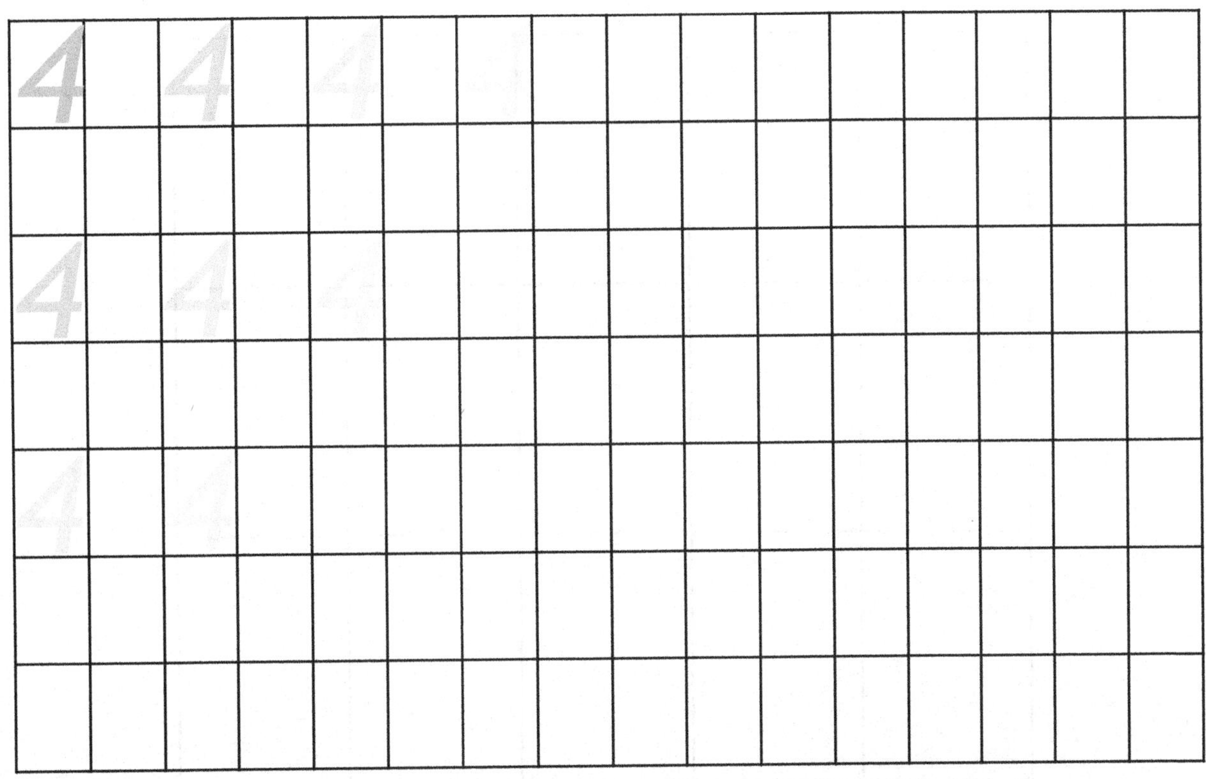

5 5 Five

Tracing & Writing 1-5

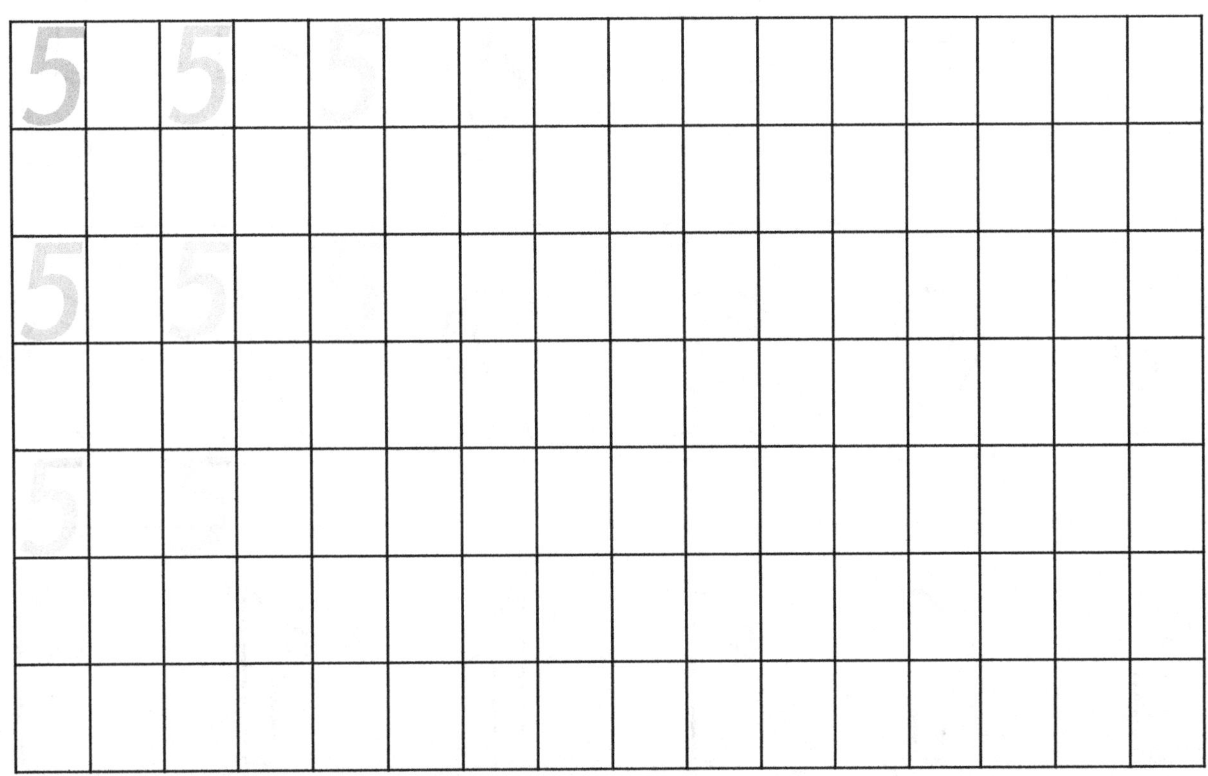

Trace the numbers and circle the wrong number in each row.

3	3	3	3	3	3
4	4	4	4	4	4
5	5	5	5	5	5
2	2	2	2	2	2
1	1	1	1	1	1

Counting 1-5

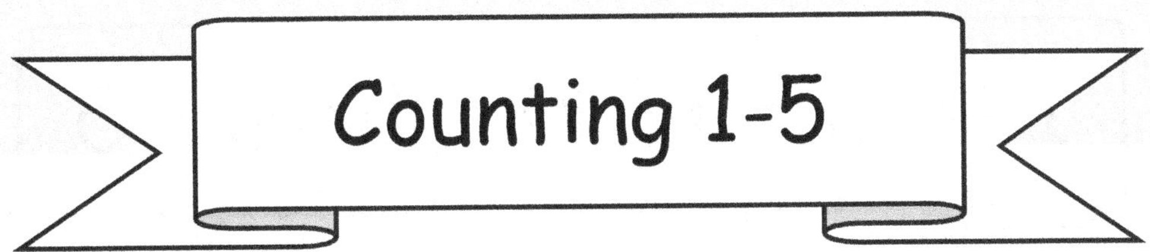

Count the objects and connect them to the right number.

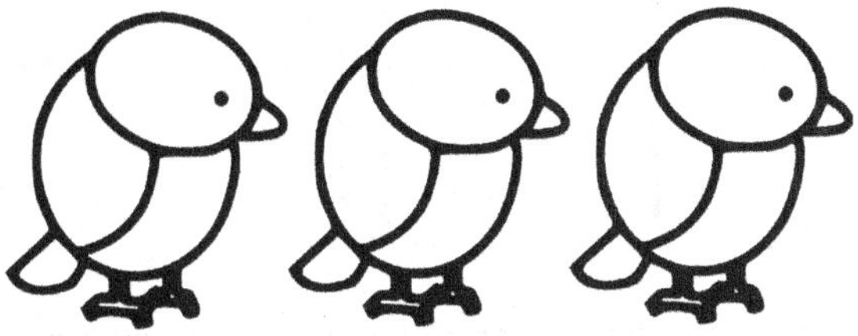

1

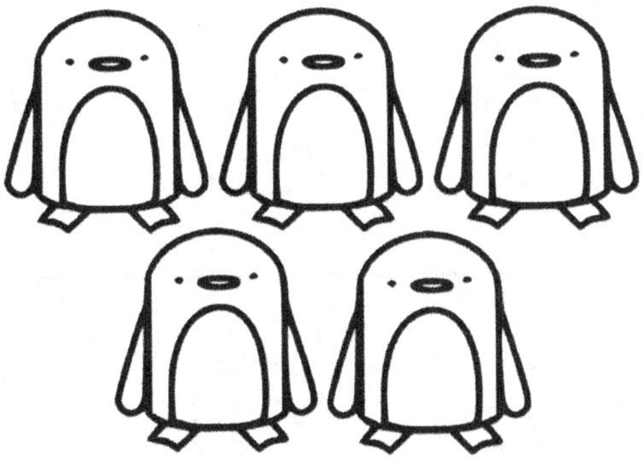

3

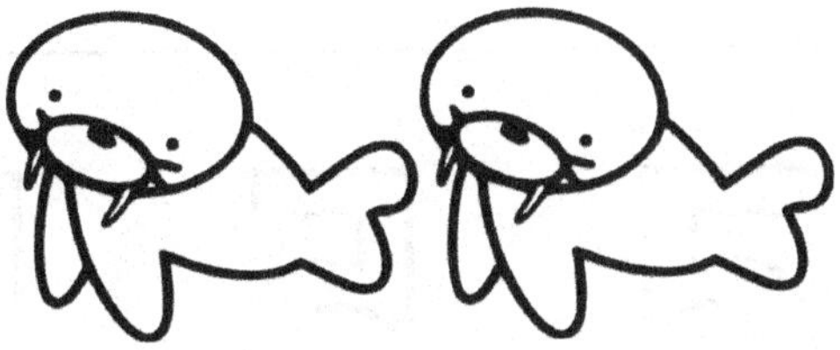

2

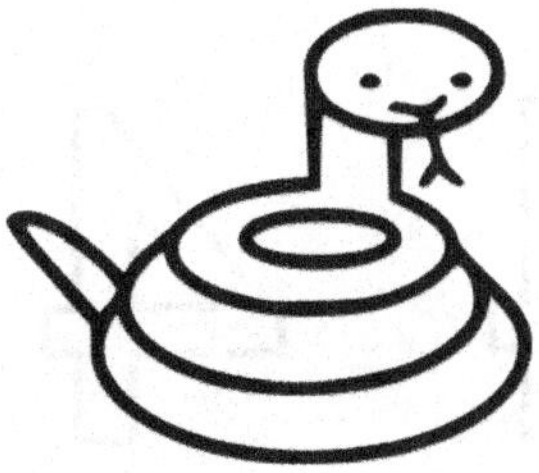

5

Identifying Numbers 1-5

Trace the numbers and circle the wrong number in each row.

Color the blocks to match the numbers.

1	2	3	4	5

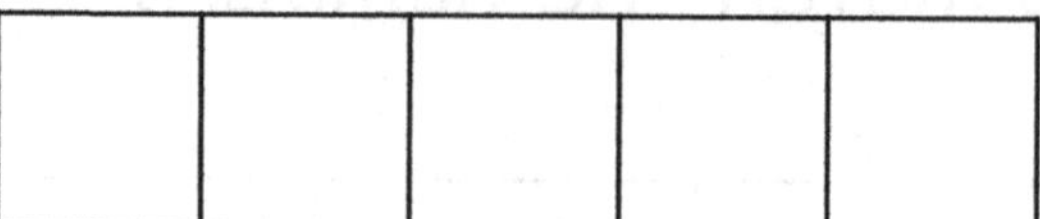

Zero

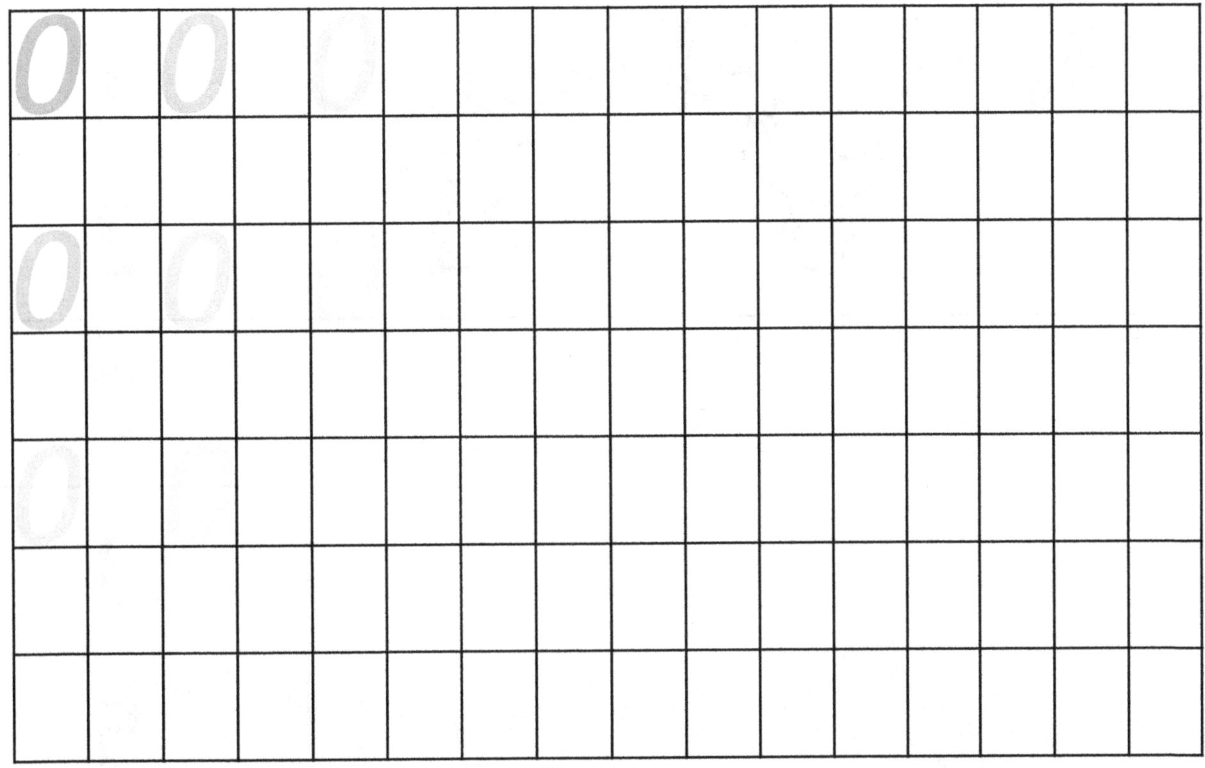

Count the objects and circle the correct number.

	1
	2
	3
	4
	1
	2
	0
	3
	5

Color the cubes that match the number in each row.

			0
			4
			1
			3

Grouping Objects 0-5

Count and circle the correct number of objects in each row.

Counting & Coloring 0-5

Color the dots on dominos to match the numbers.

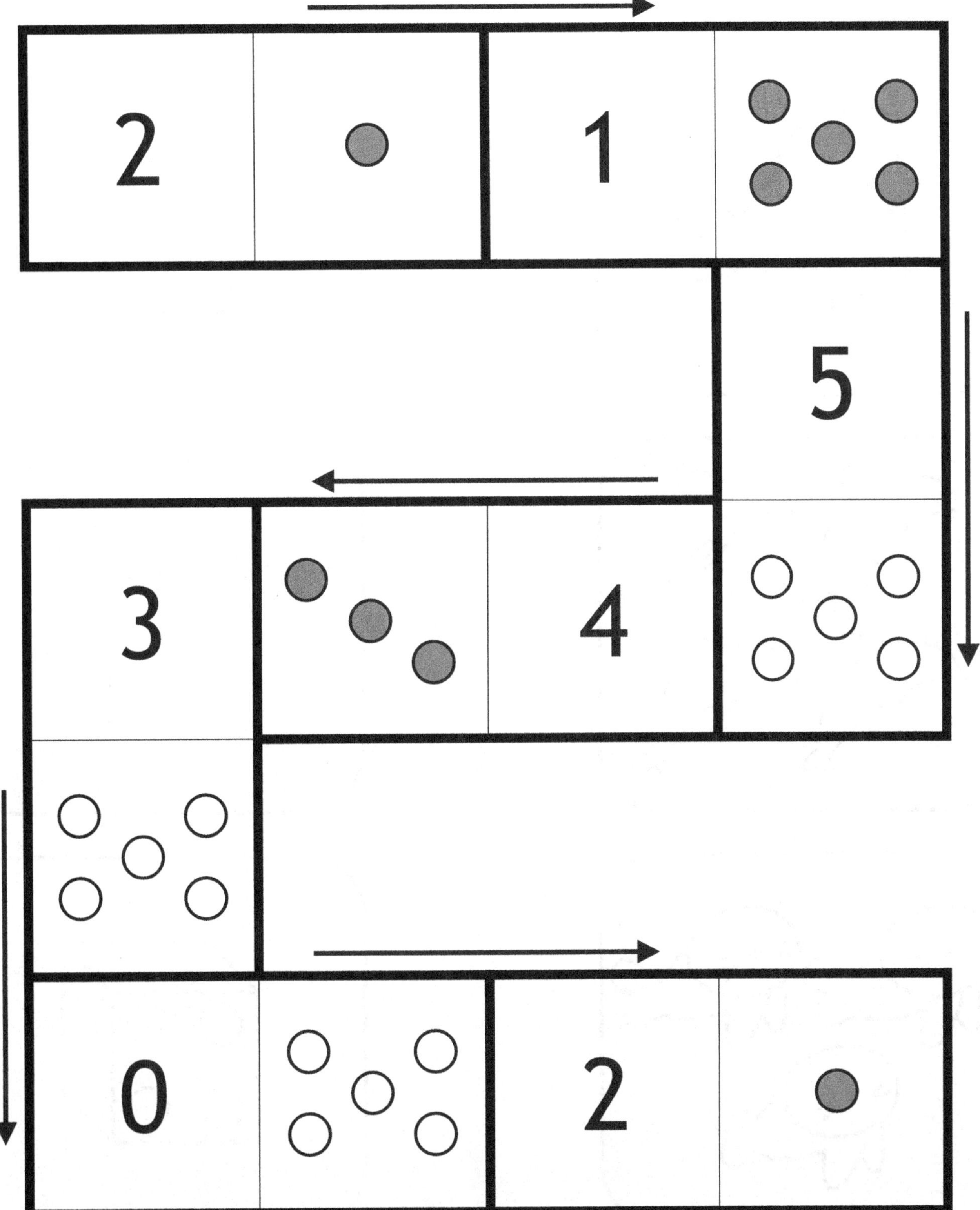

Grouping Objects 0-5

Count the objects and connect each group to the same number.

Color the blocks to match the numbers.

1	3	5	2	4	0

Counting & Coloring 0-5

Color the cubes that match the number in each row.

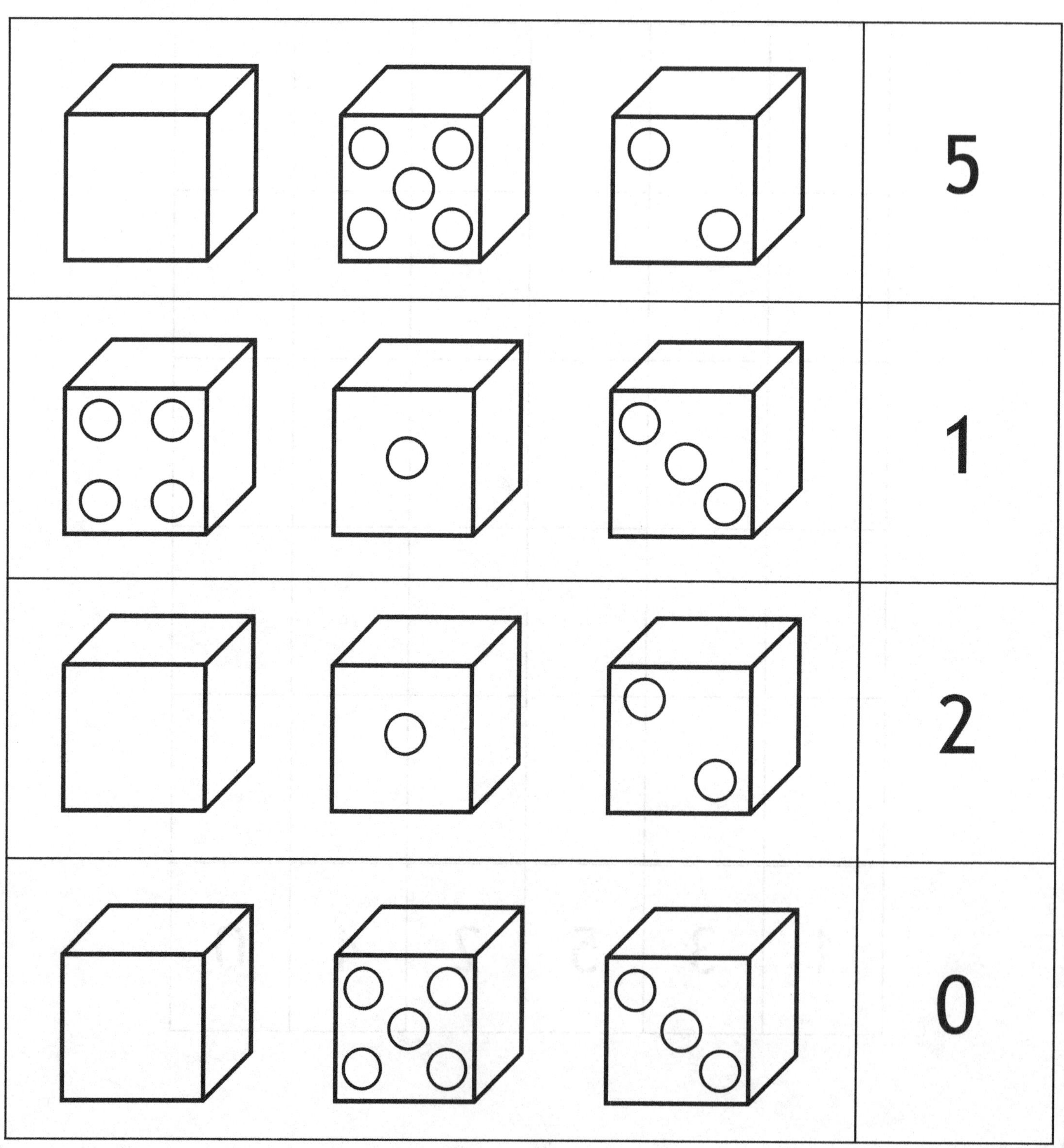

Grouping Objects 0-5

Count and circle the correct number of objects in each row.

Color the dots on dominos to match the numbers.

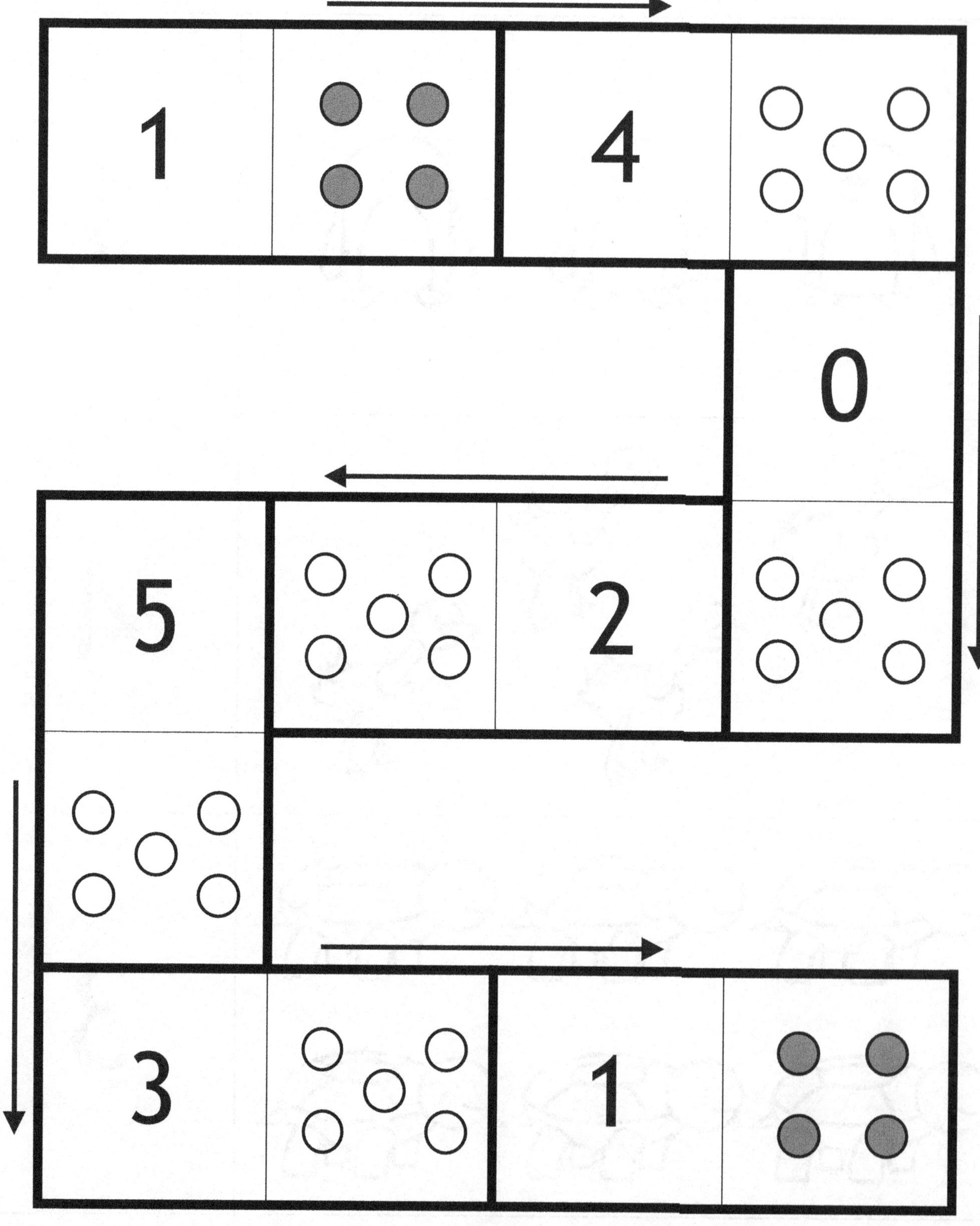

Grouping Objects to 0-5

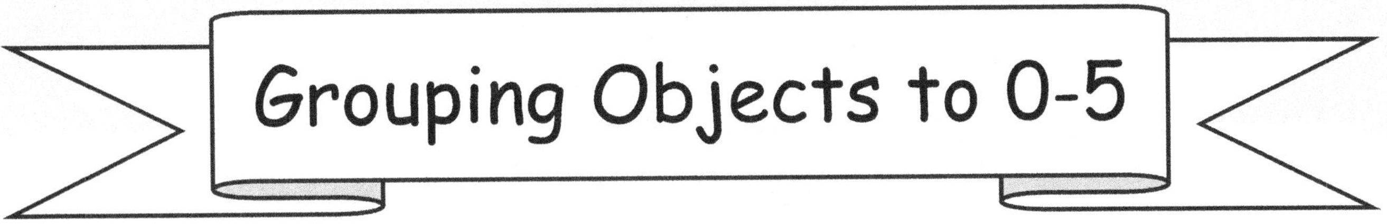

Count the objects and connect each group to the same number.

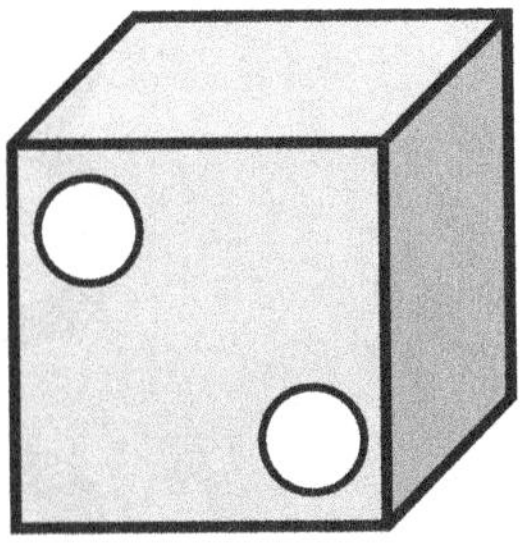

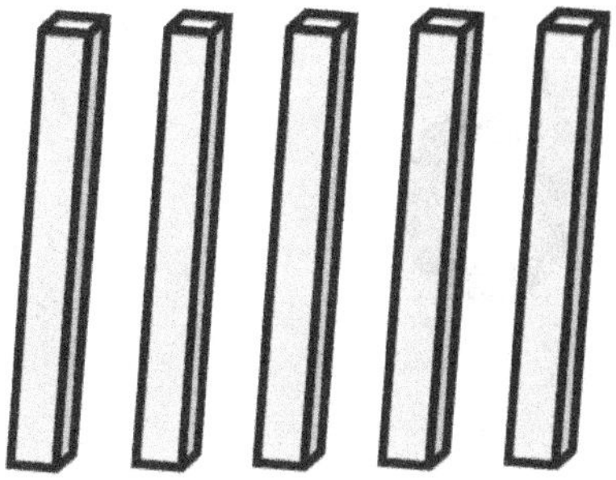

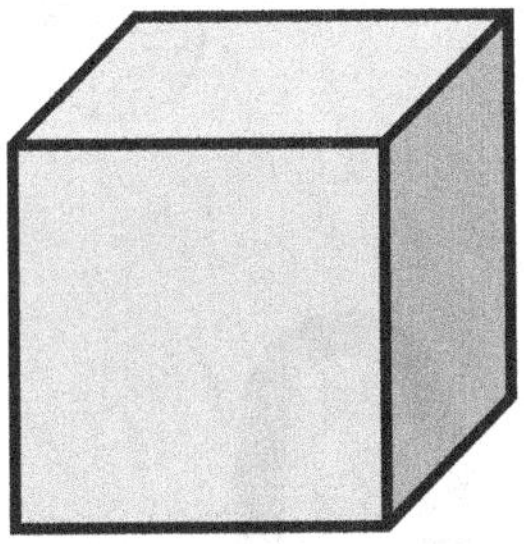

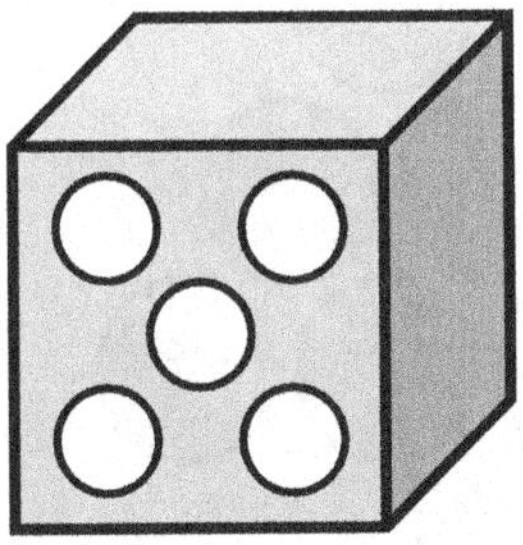

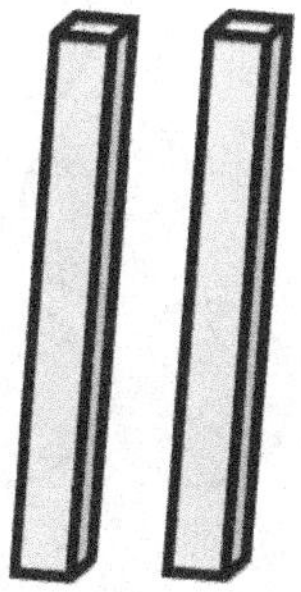

6

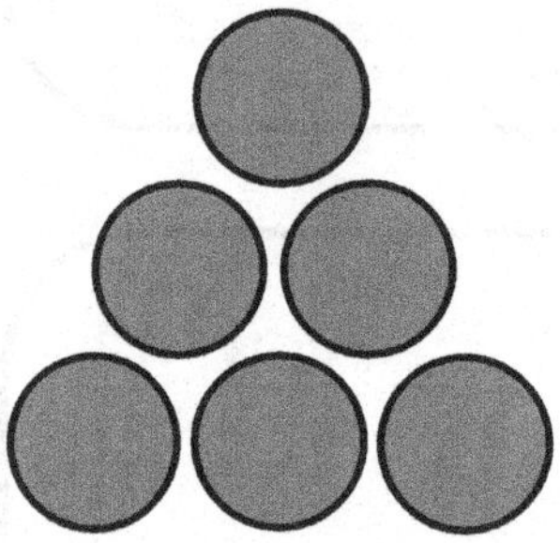

7

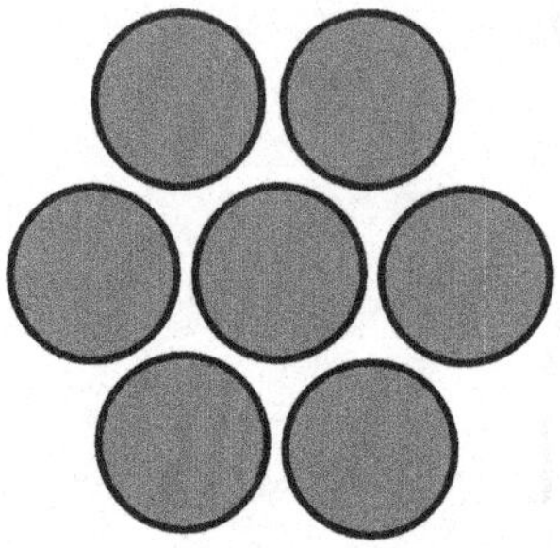

8

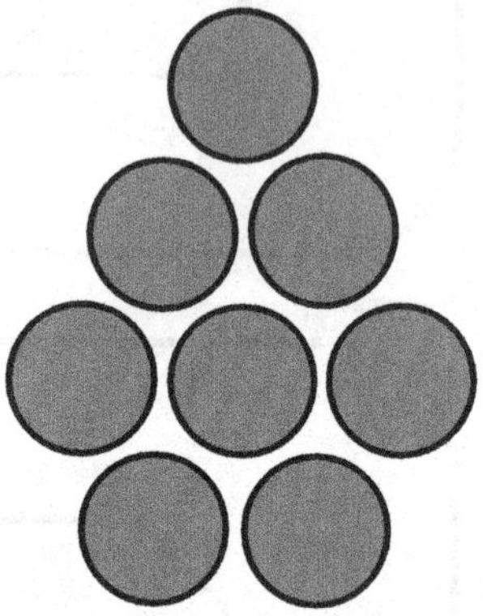

9

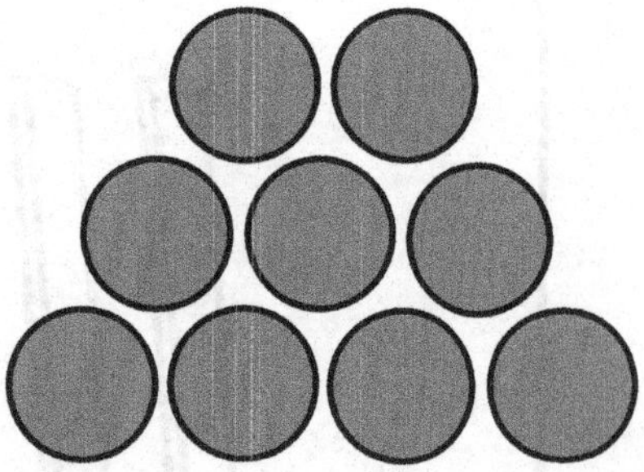

10

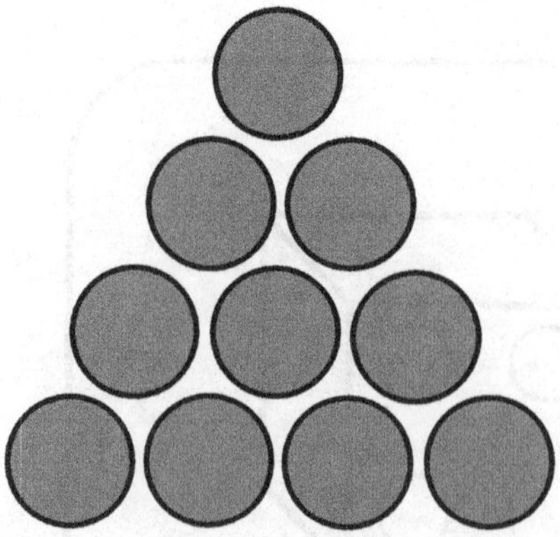

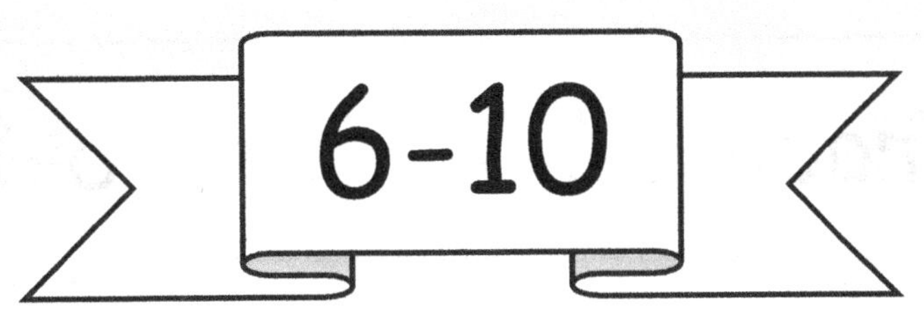

6
Six

7
Seven

8
Eight

9
Nine

10
Ten

6 6 *Six*

Tracing & Writing 6-10

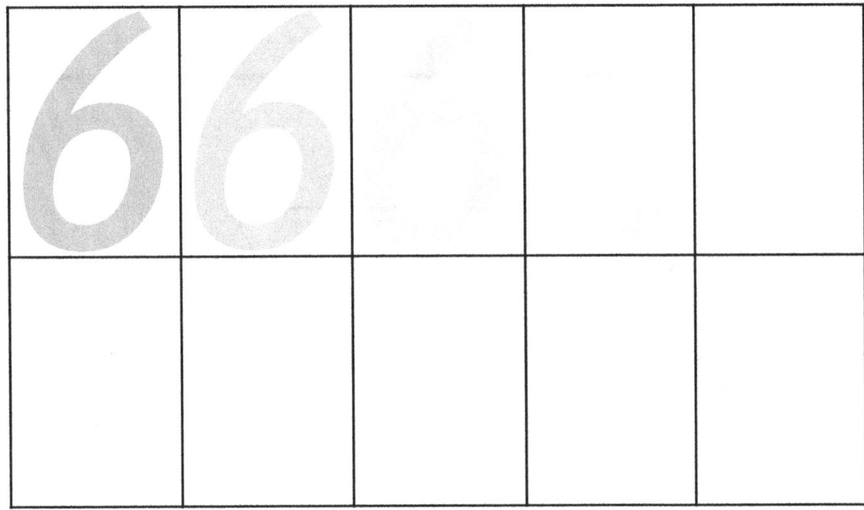

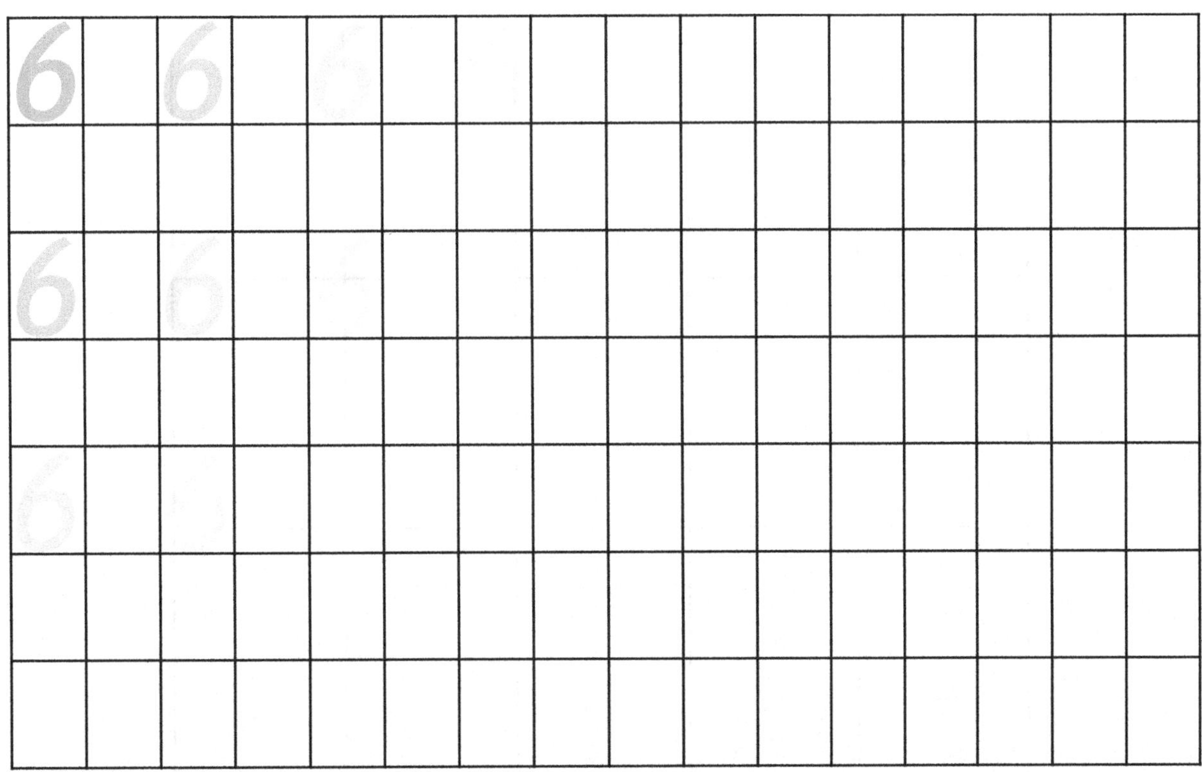

7 7 Seven

37

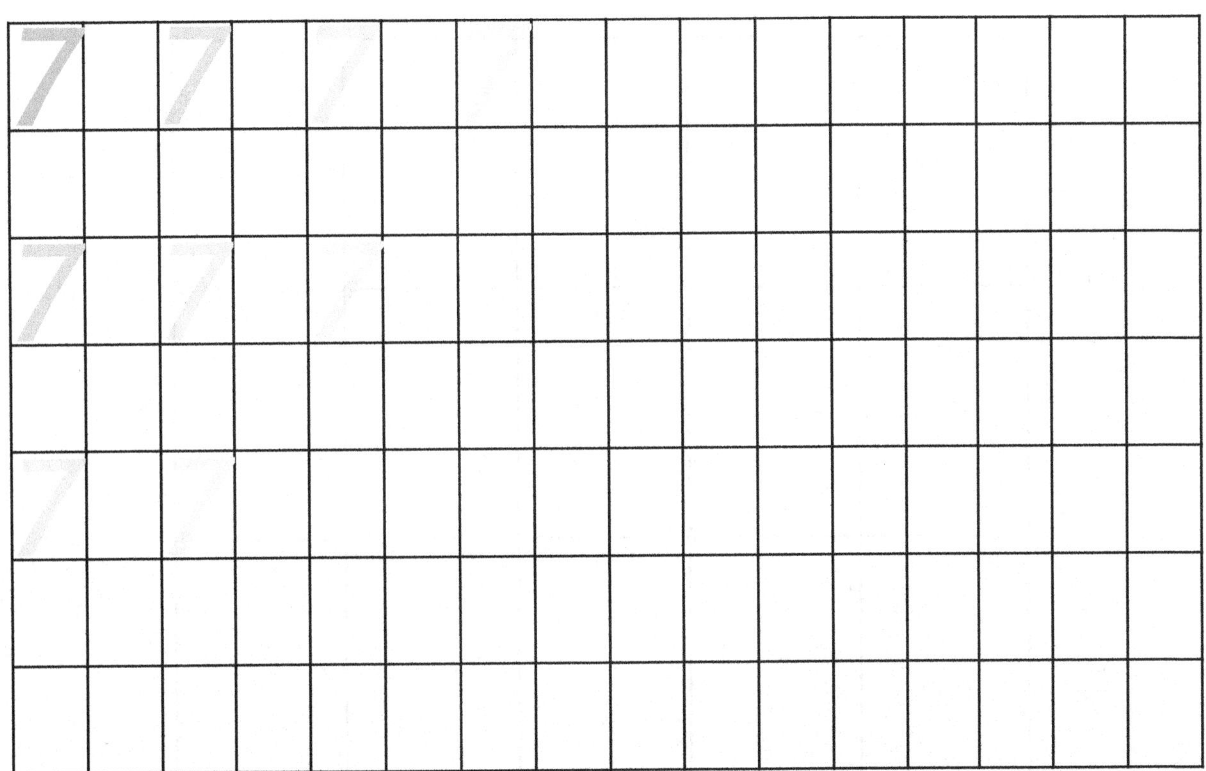

8 8 *Eight*

Tracing & Writing 6-10

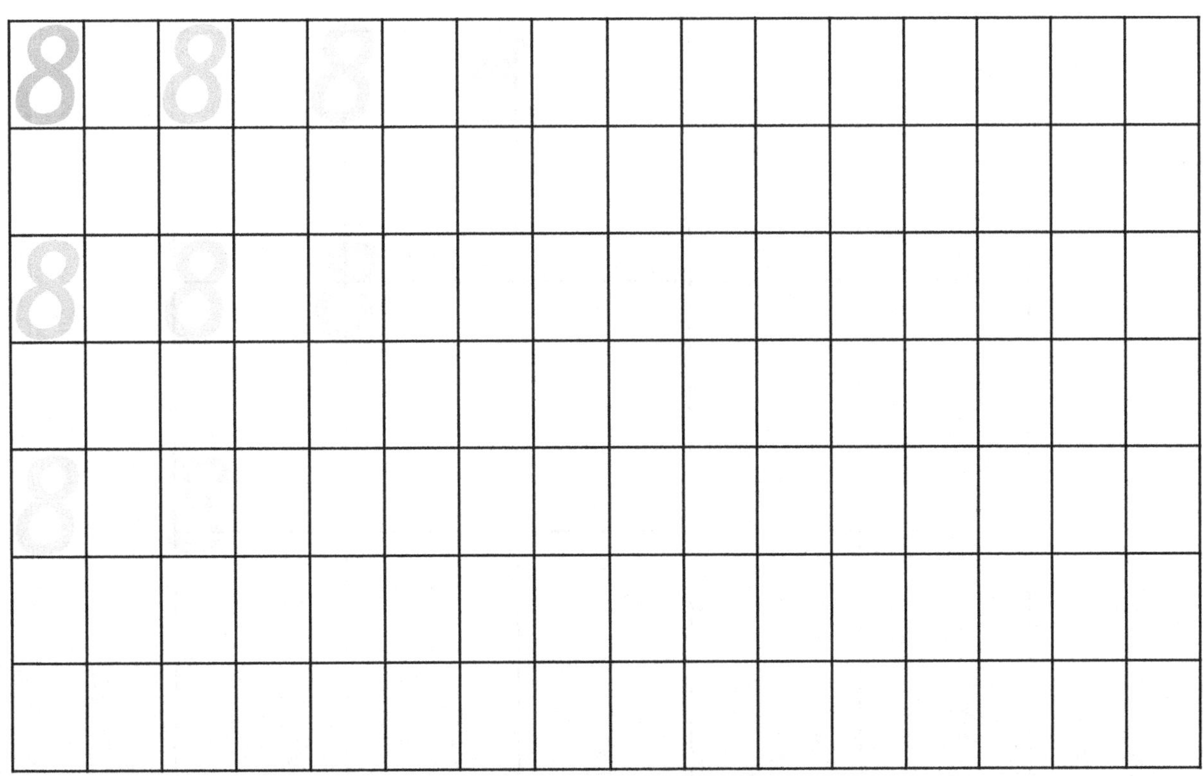

9 9 Nine

Tracing & Writing 6-10

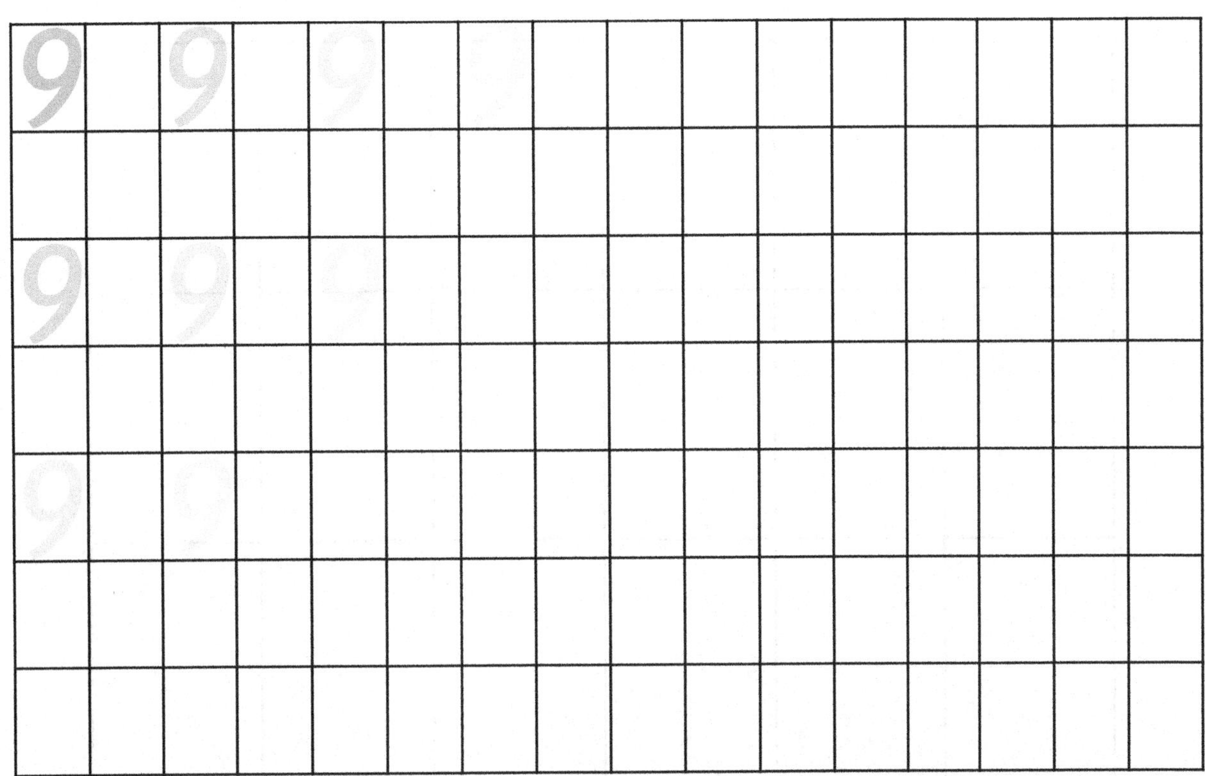

Ten

Tracing & Writing 6-10

10 10

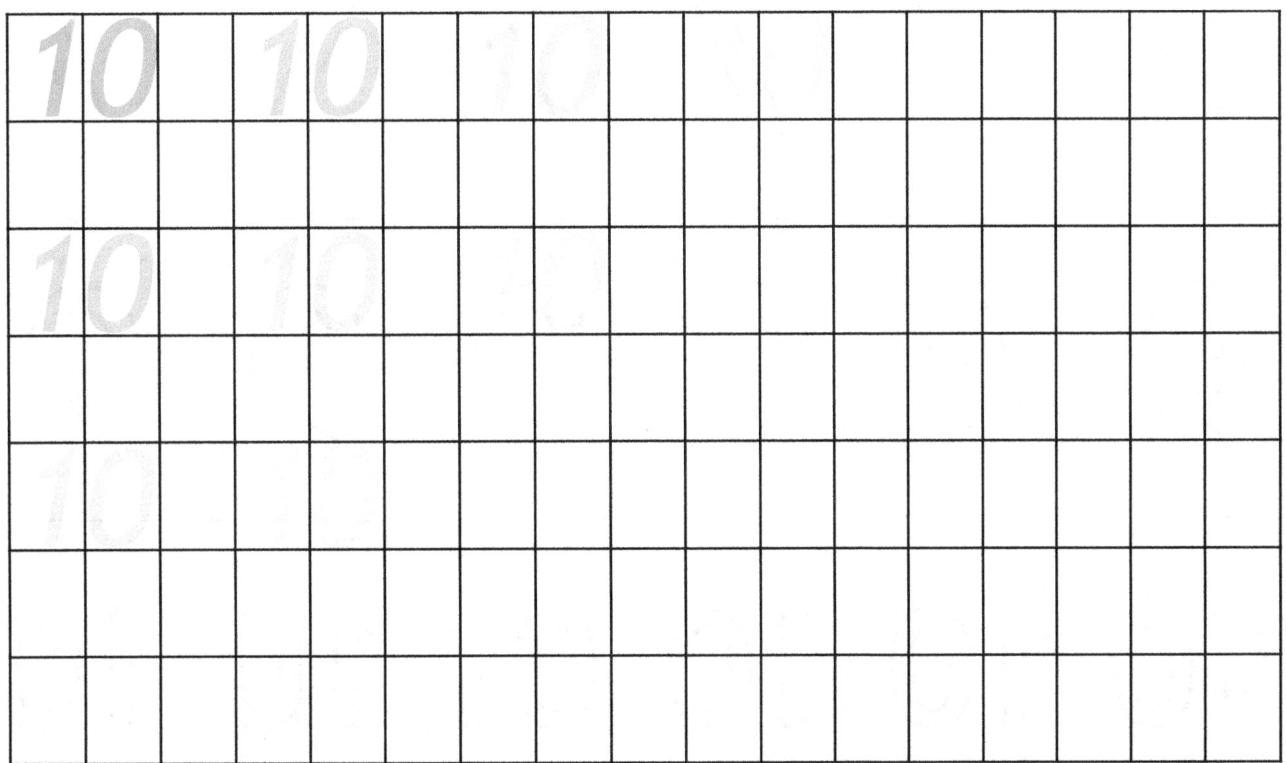

10 10
10 10
10

Identifying Numbers 6-10

Trace the numbers and circle the wrong number in each row.

- Row 1 (8): 8 8 8 8 8 8
- Row 2 (6): 6 6 6 6 6 6
- Row 3 (7): 7 7 7 7 7 7
- Row 4 (9): 9 9 9 9 9 9
- Row 5 (10): 10 10 10 10 10 10

Count the objects and connect them to the right number.

10

8

7

9

Identifying Numbers 6-10

Trace the numbers and circle the wrong number in each row.

10	10	10	10	ſ0	10
8	8	8	8	8	∞
9	9	℮	9	9	9
7	7	7	⊽	7	7
6	∂	6	6	6	6

Count the objects and circle the correct number.

	10
	8
	6
	7
	9
	6
	7
	8
	9

Color the blocks to match the numbers.

6	7	8	9	10

Grouping Objects 6-10

Count and circle the correct number of objects in each row.

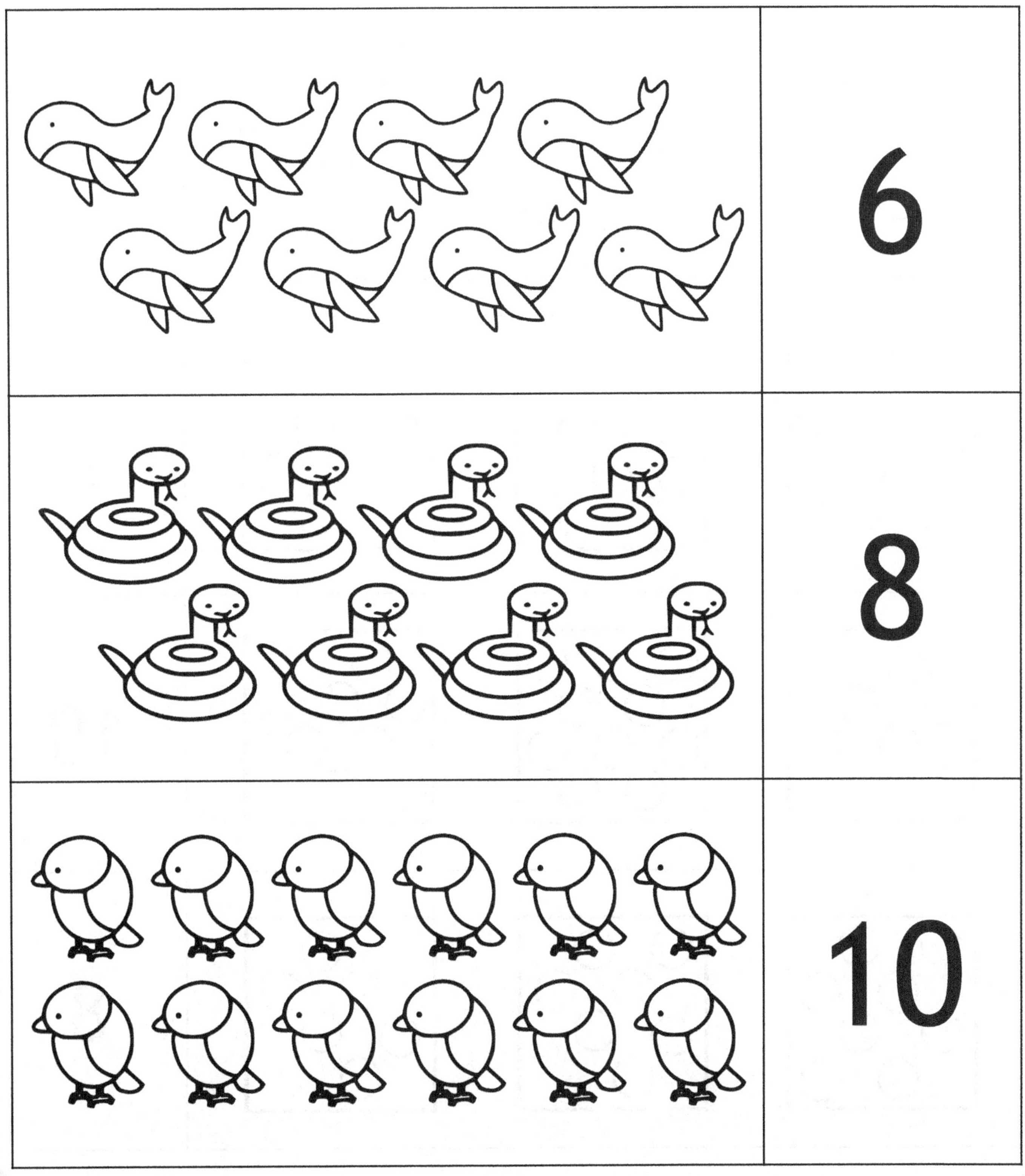

Color the squares that match the number in each row.

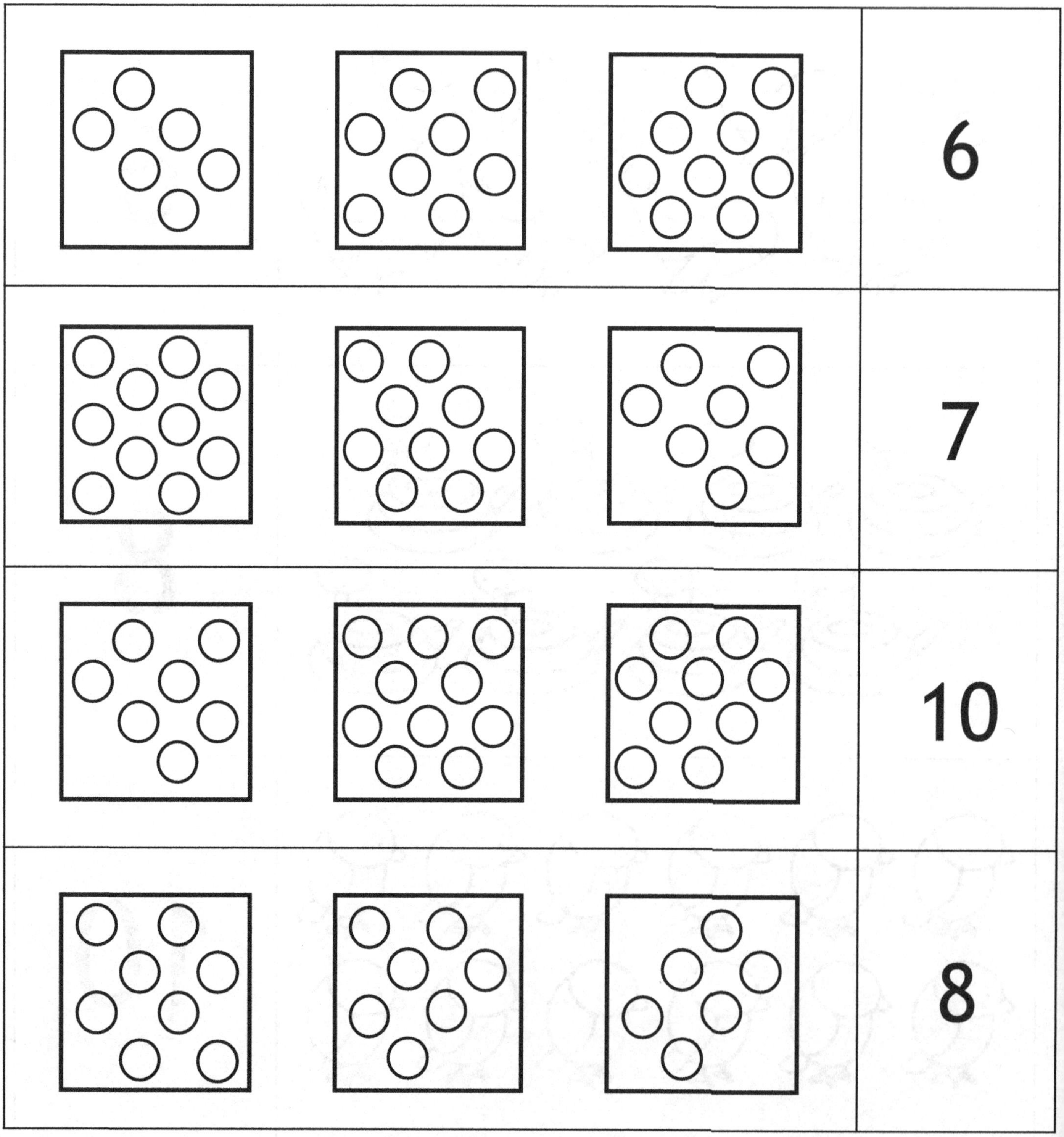

			6
			7
			10
			8

Counting & Coloring 6-10

Color the ten frames on dominos to match the numbers.

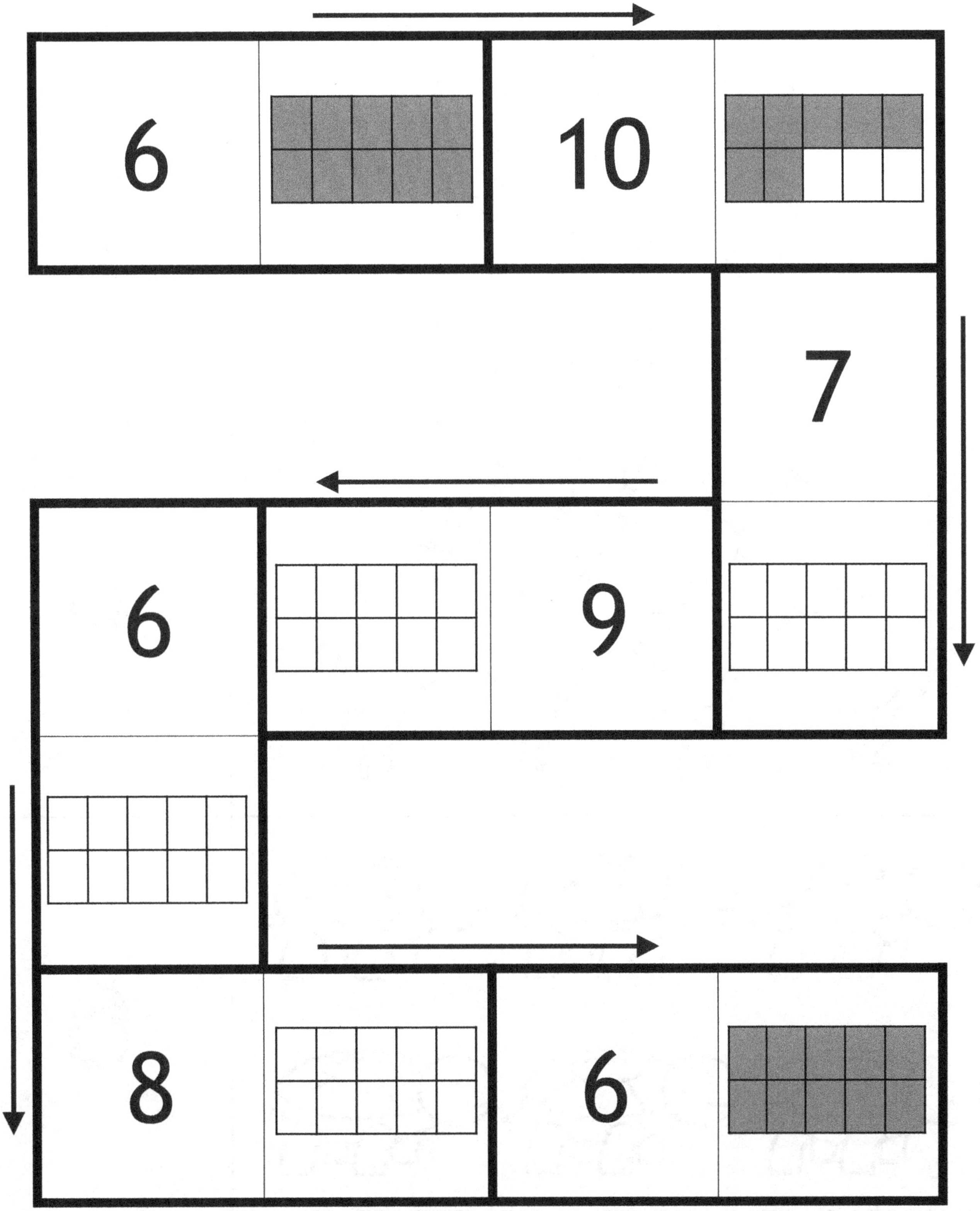

6   10

7

6   9

8   6

Grouping Objects 6-10

Count and circle the correct number of objects in each row.

	7
	9
	6

Color the blocks to match the numbers.

6	9	10	7	8

Color the squares that match the number in each row.

			9
			8
			7
			6

Grouping Objects to 6-10

Count the objects and connect each group to the same number.

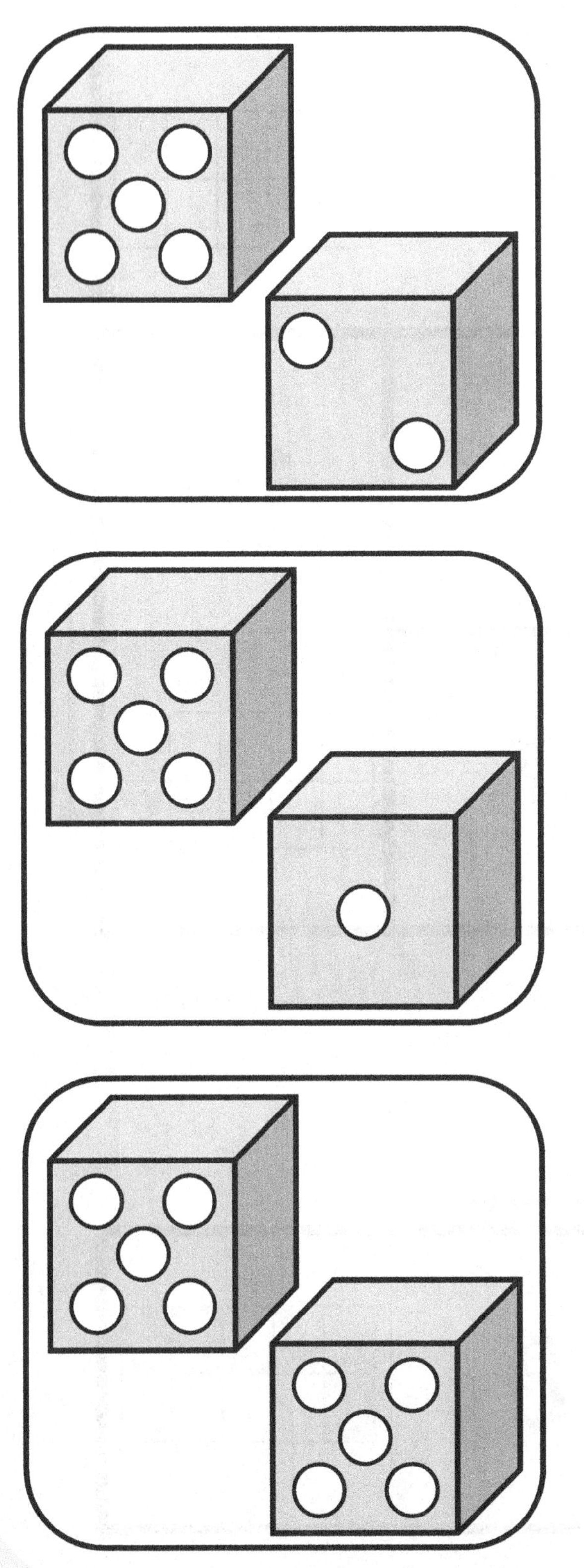

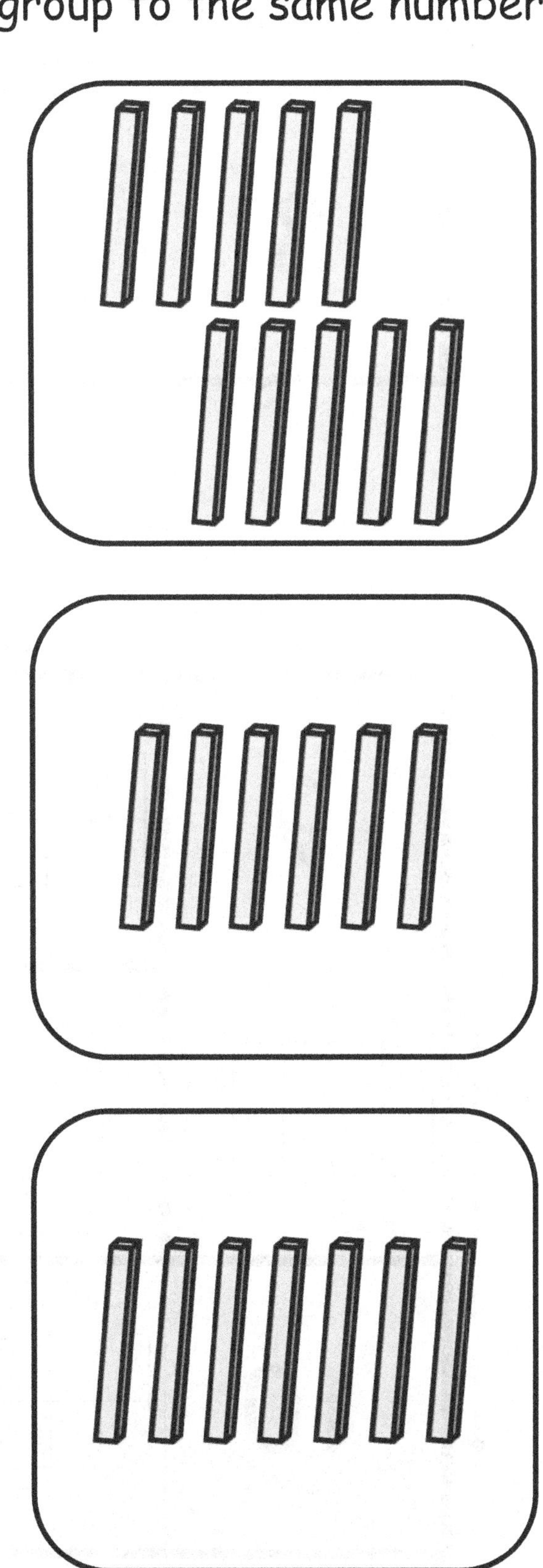

Counting & Coloring 6-10

Color the ten frames on dominos to match the numbers.

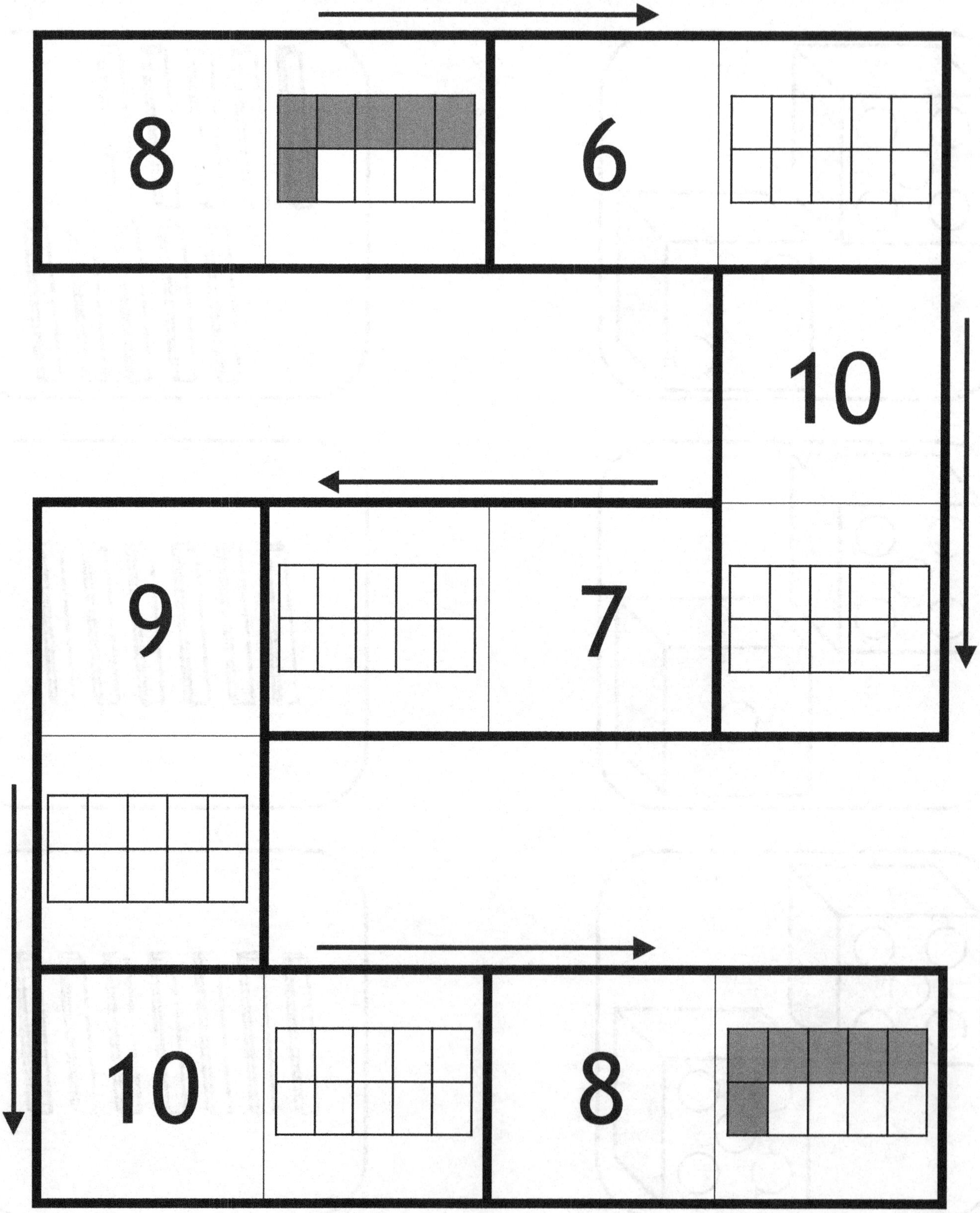

8

6

10

9

7

10

8

Paste the missing numbers in each row.

Ordering Numbers to 10

Paste the missing numbers in each row.

| 7 | 8 | | 10 |

| 3 | | 5 | 6 |

| 5 | | 7 | 8 |

- ✂

| 6 | 9 | 4 |

Paste the missing numbers in each row.

Ordering Numbers to 10

Paste the missing numbers in each row.

| 1 | 2 | | 4 |

| | 7 | 8 | 9 |

| 4 | 5 | 6 | |

| 3 | 4 | | 6 |

| 5 | 3 | 6 | 7 |

Ordering Numbers to 10

Order the numbers and color the balls by numbers.

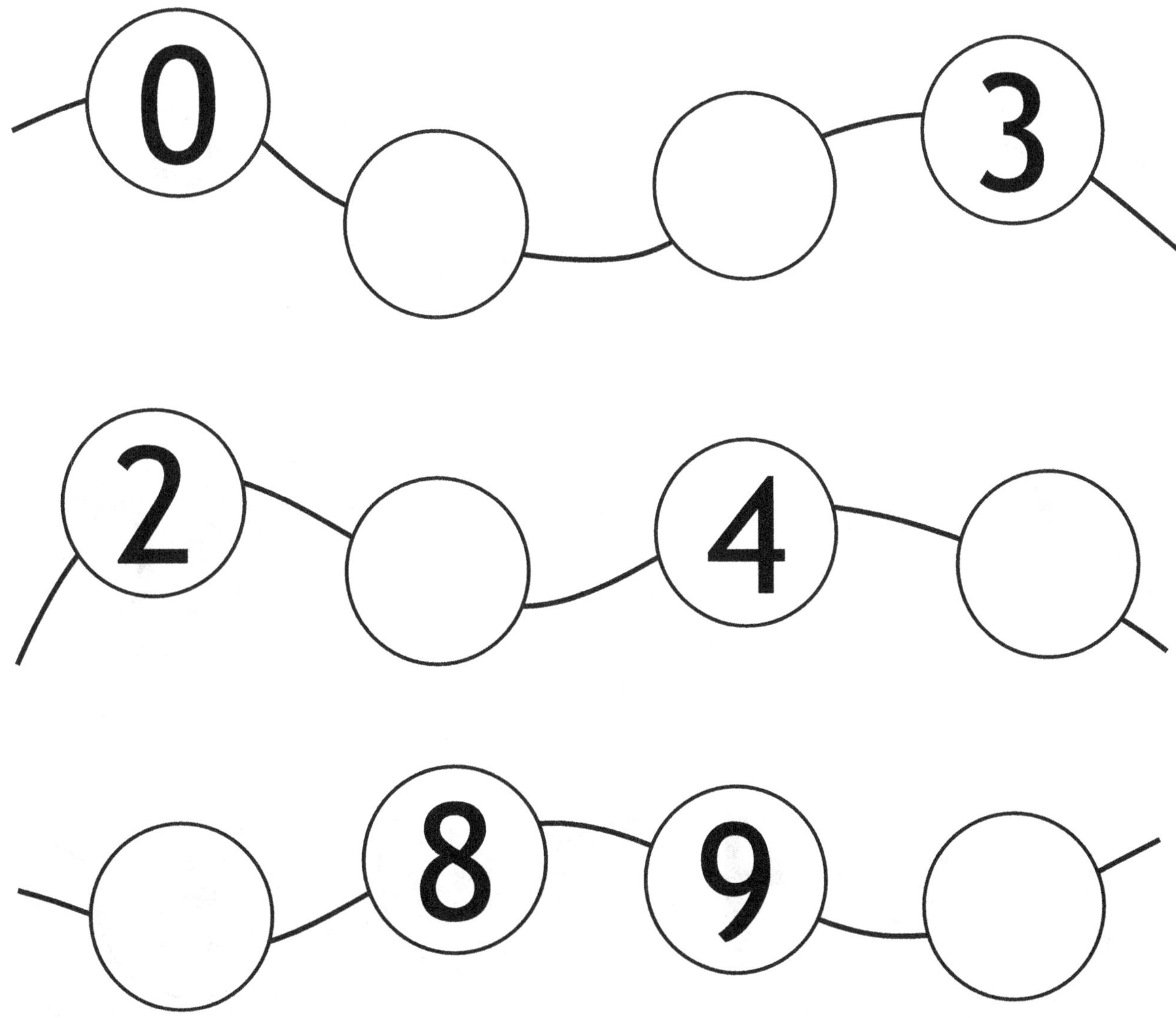

0 yellow 1 blue 2 red 3 purple 4 green 5 orange

6 brown 7 pink 8 grey 9 black 10 white

Ordering Numbers to 10

Order the numbers and color the balls by numbers.

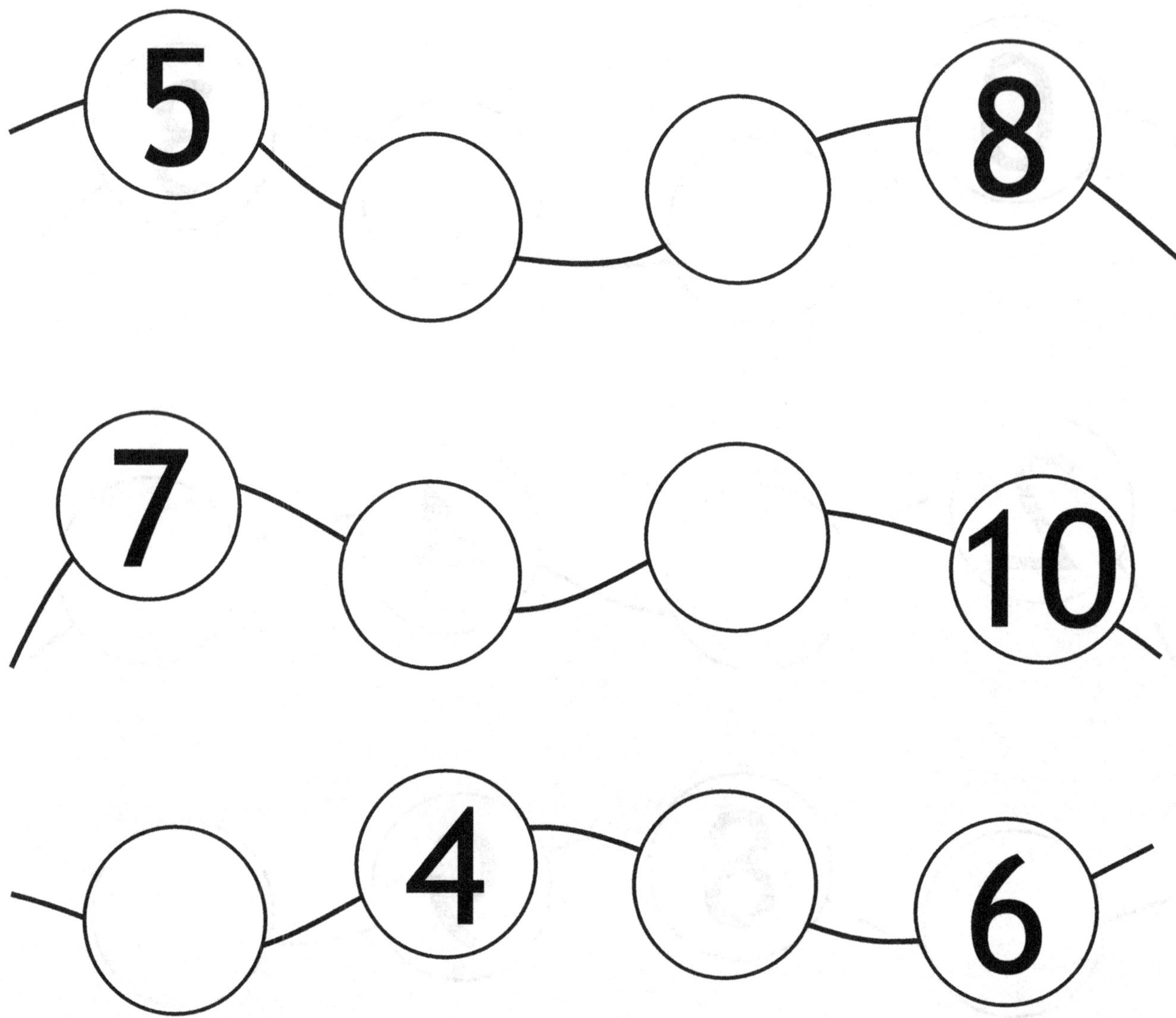

0 yellow   1 blue   2 red   3 purple   4 green   5 orange

6 brown   7 pink   8 grey   9 black   10 white

Coloring by Numbers

Color by numbers.

1 blue   2 red   3 yellow   4 green   5 orange

Coloring by Numbers

Color by numbers.

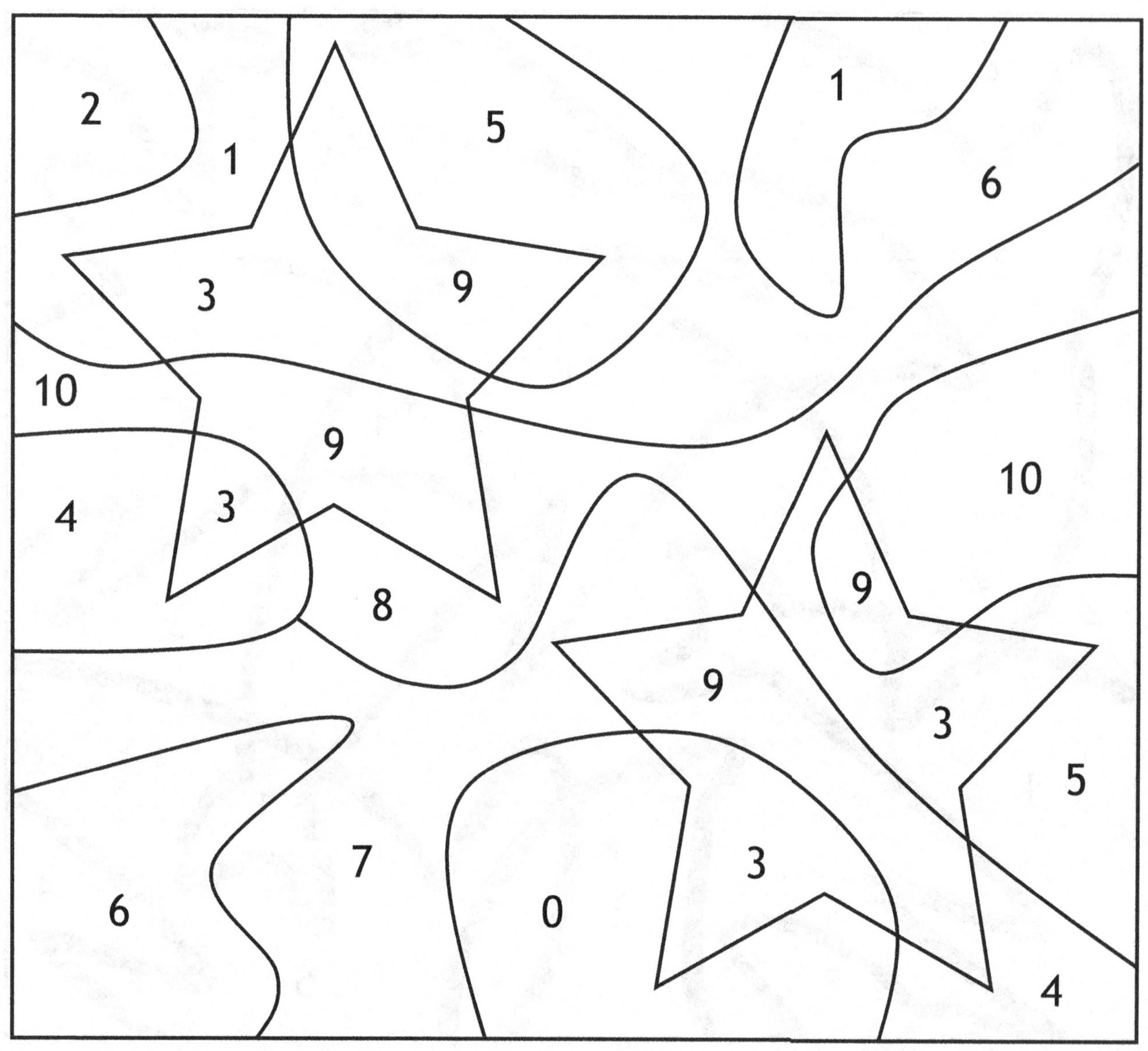

1	blue	2	green	3	yellow
4	orange	5	red	6	purple
7	blue	8	green	9	yellow
10	orange	0	red		

Comparing Numbers & Objects

Color the cube that has more dots than the number.

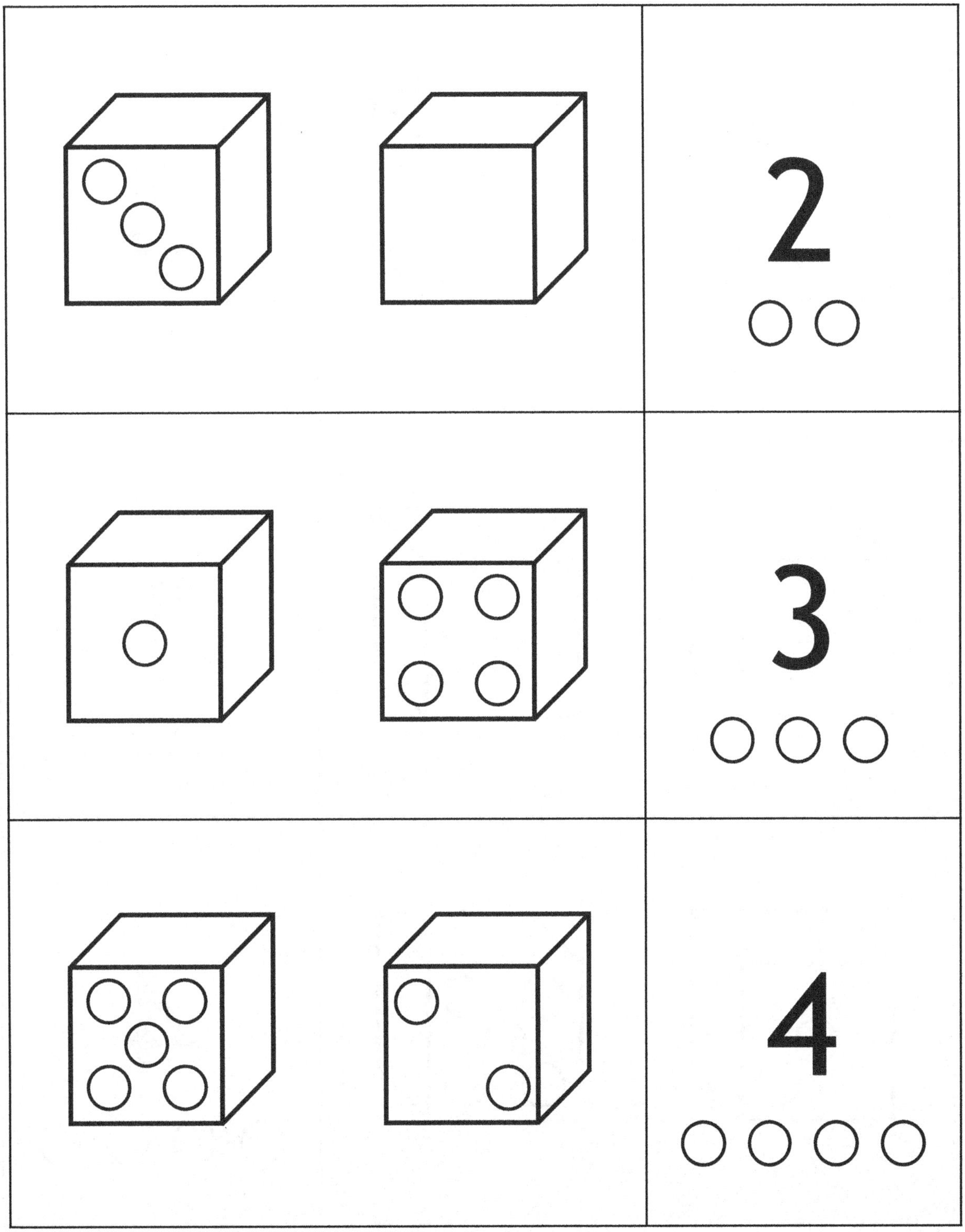

67

Comparing Numbers & Objects

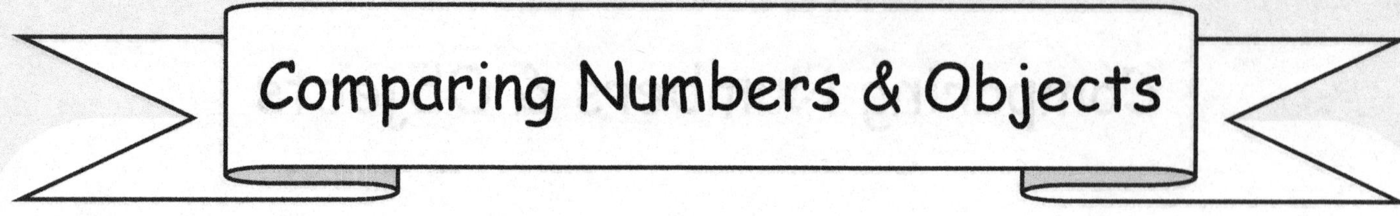

Color the cube that has less dots than the number.

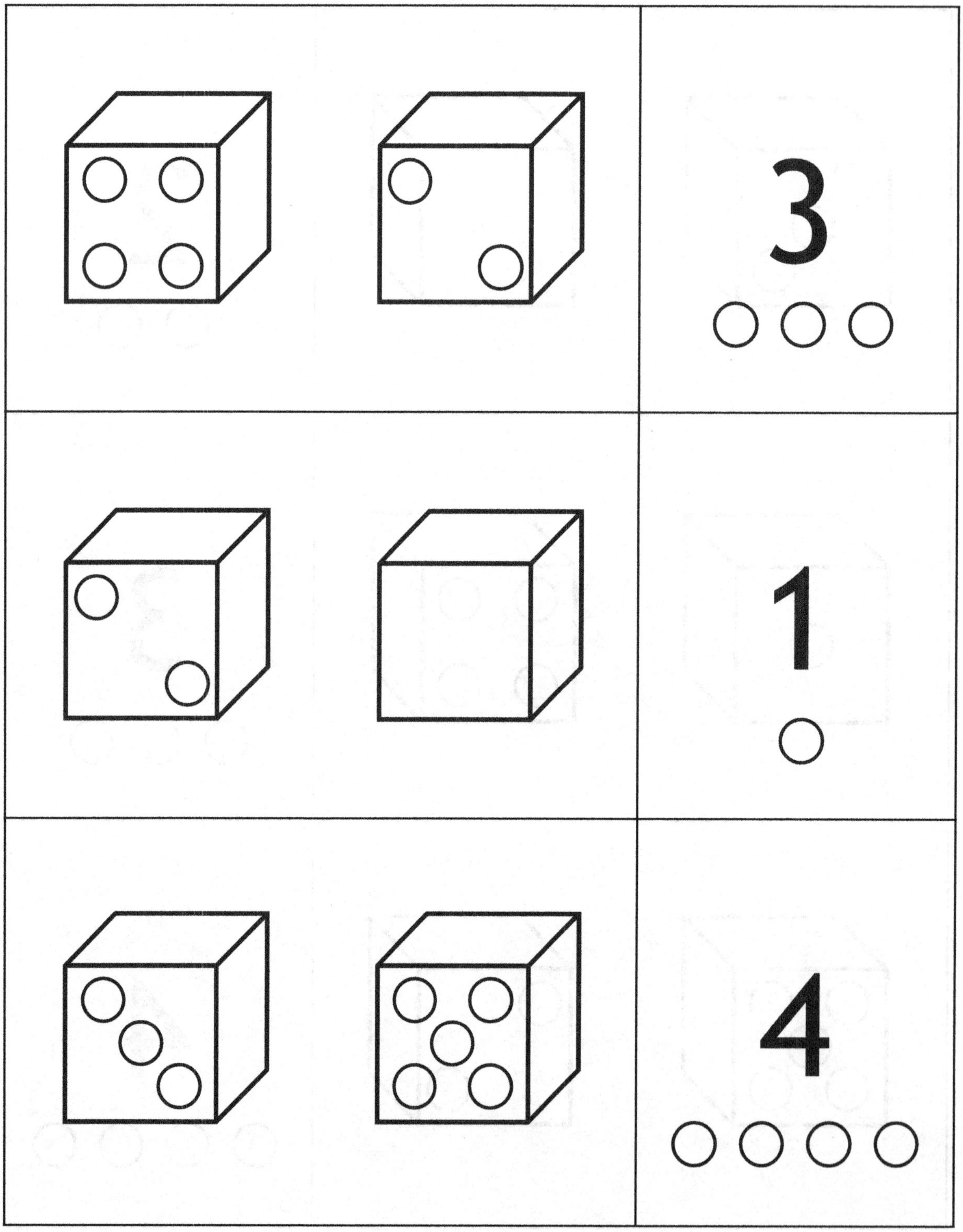

Comparing Numbers & Objects

Color the cube that has the most dots in each row.

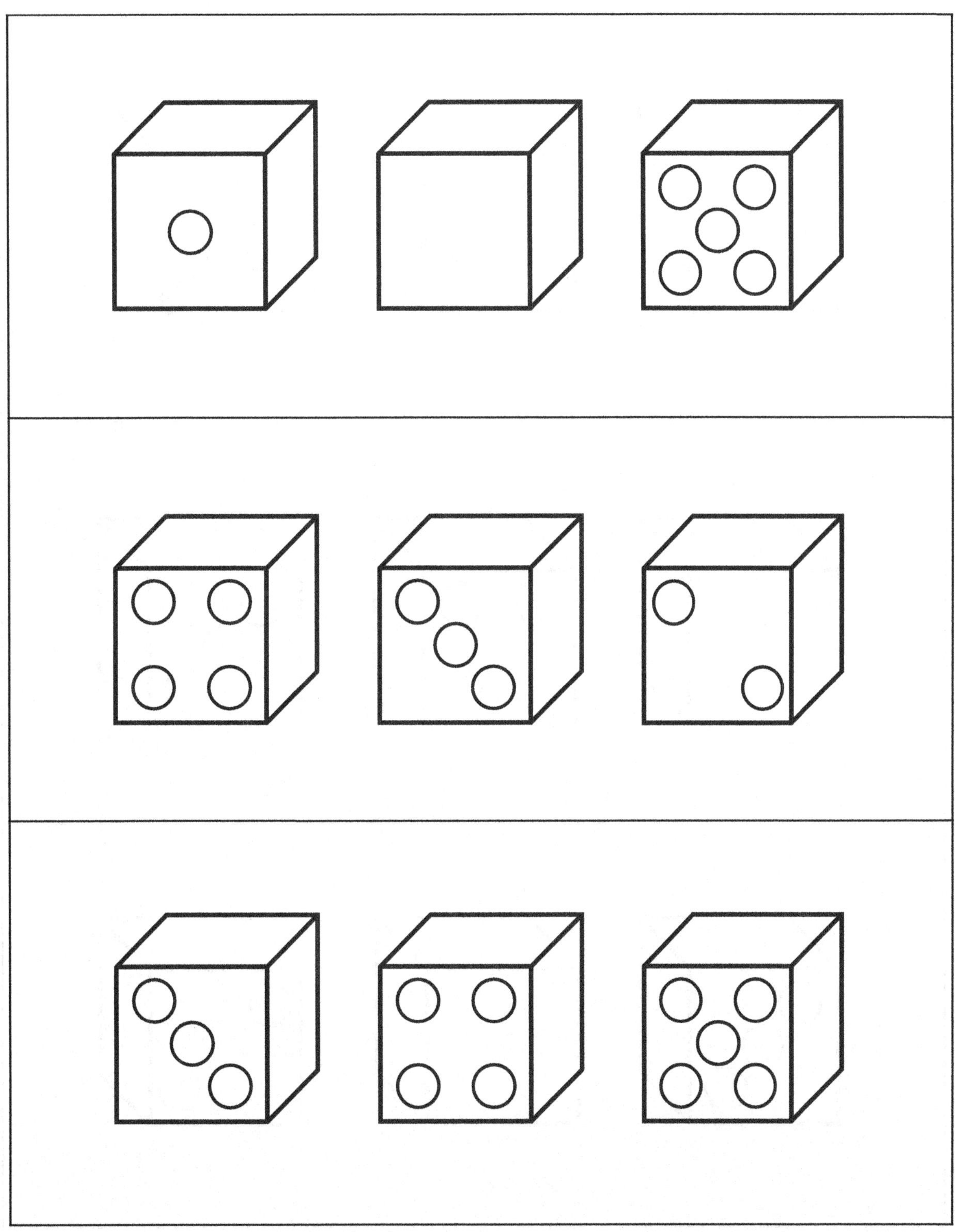

Comparing Numbers & Objects

Color the cube that has the less dots in each row.

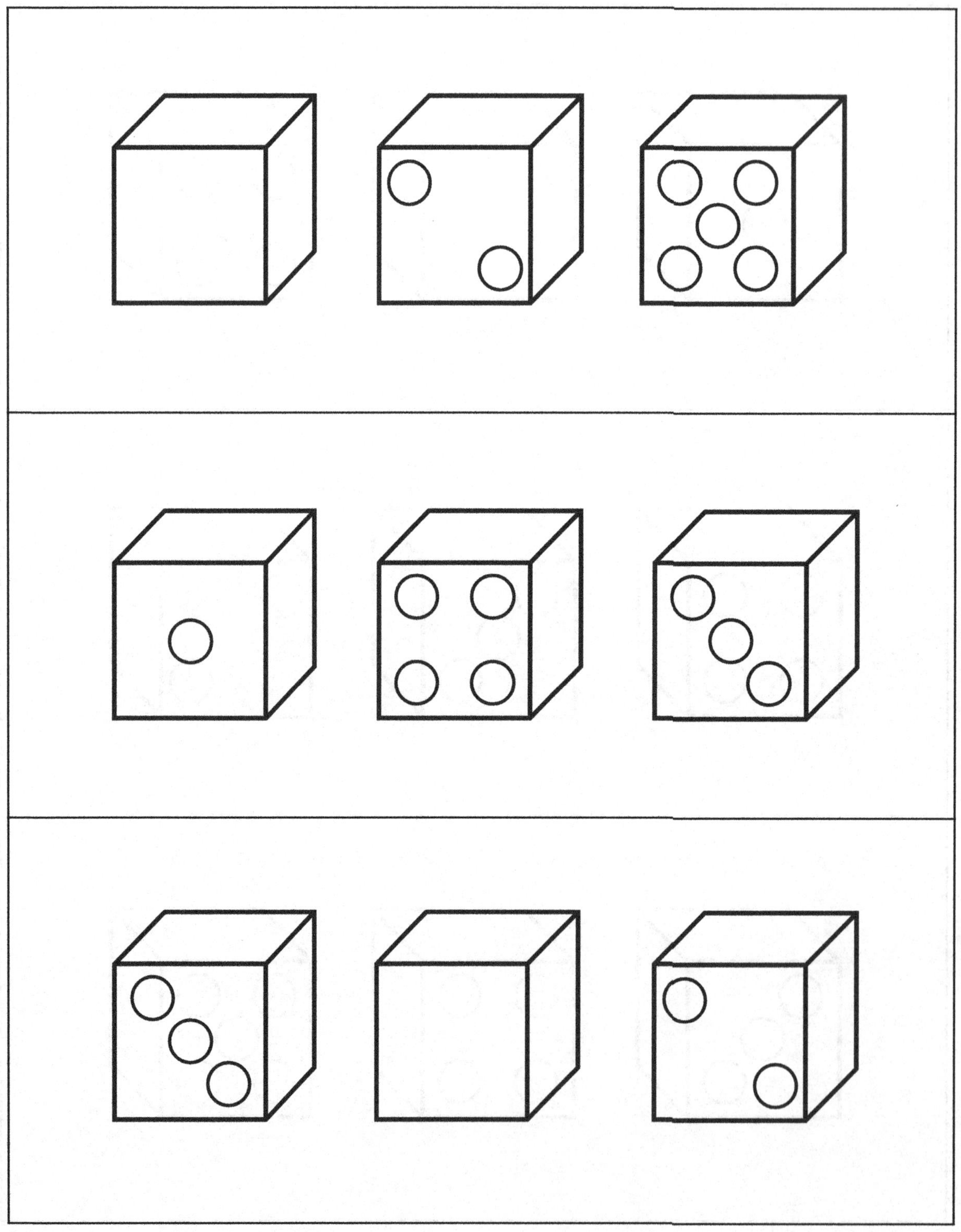

Comparing Numbers & Objects

Color the square that has the most dots in each row.

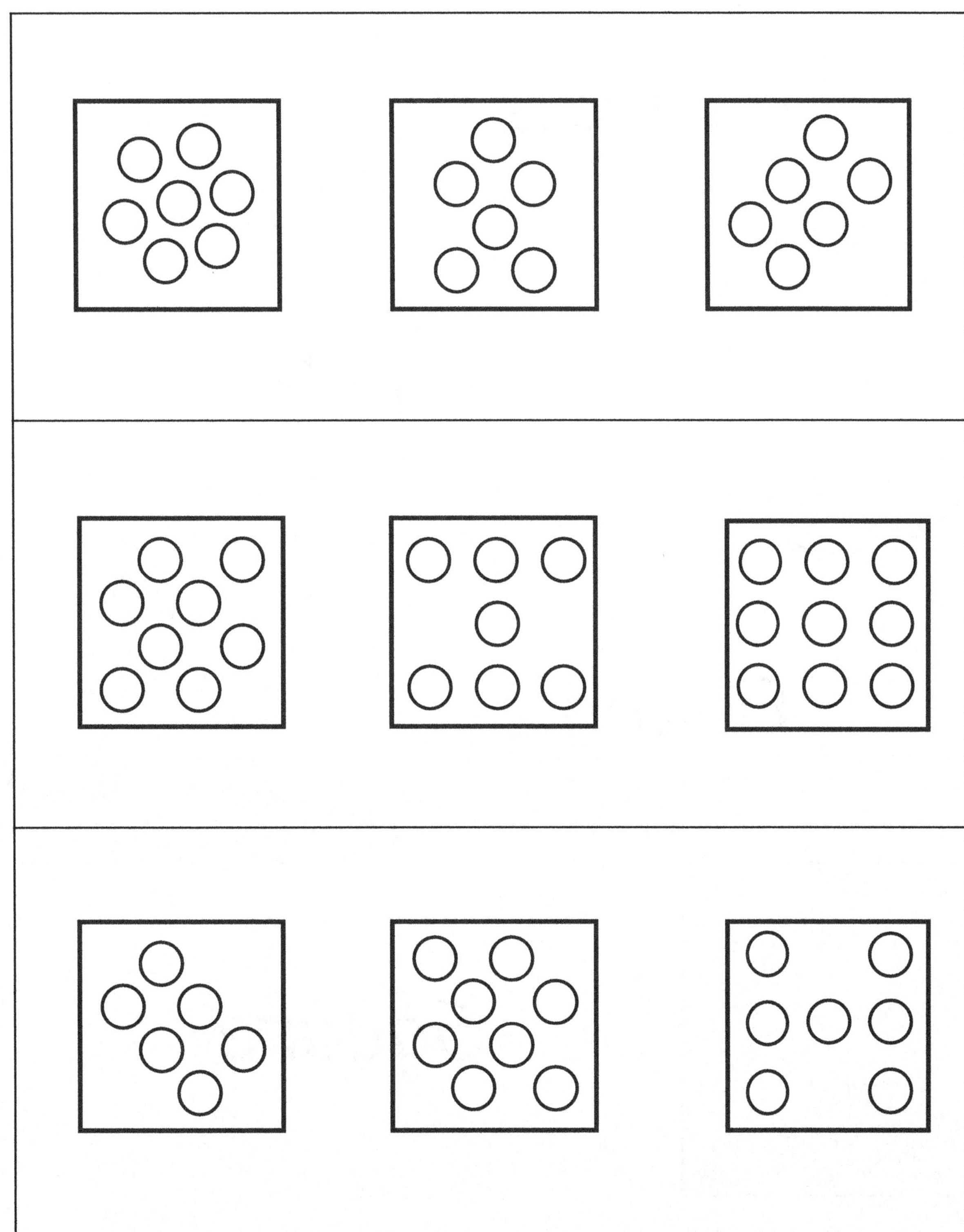

Rectangle

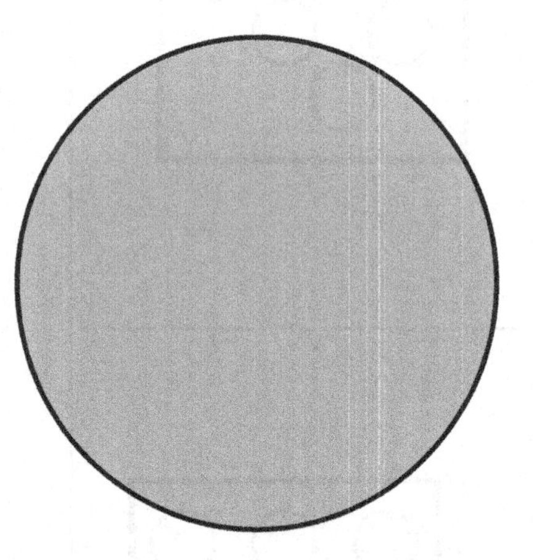

Circle

Triangle

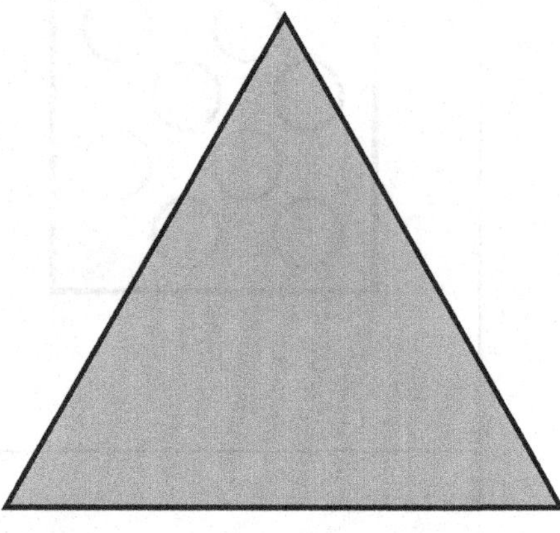

Square

Tracing the Shapes

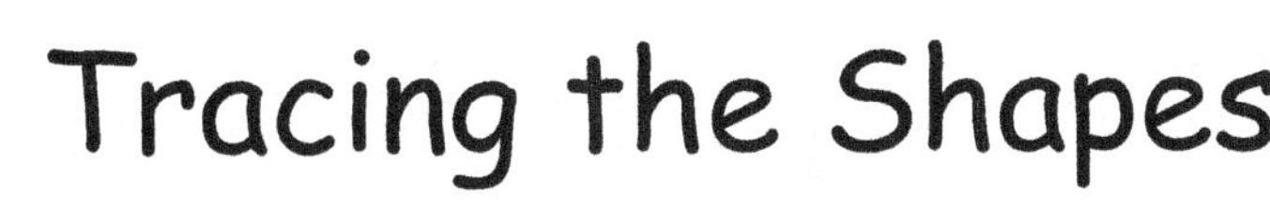

Rectangle

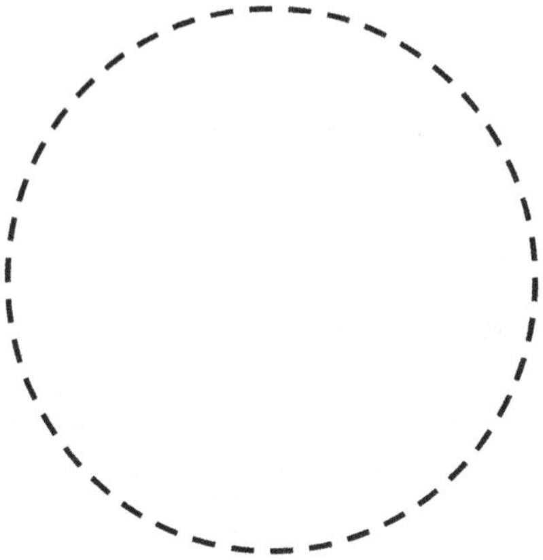

Circle

Triangle

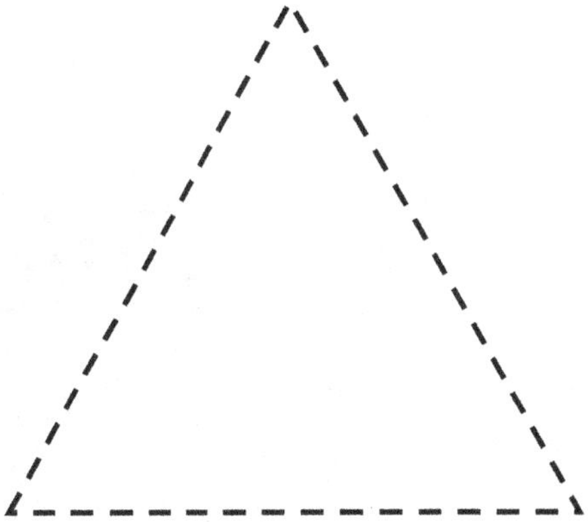

Square

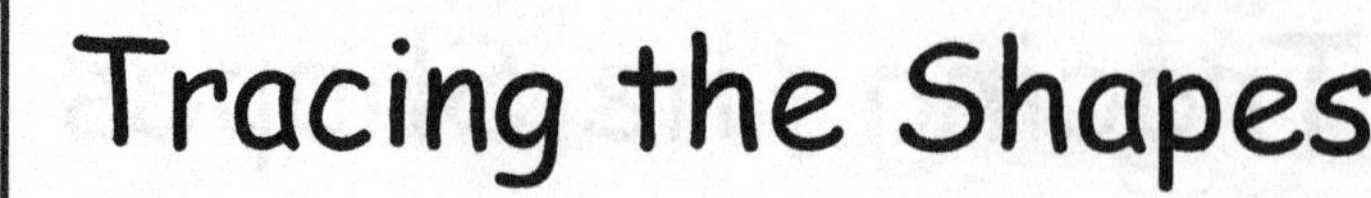

Rectangle

Circle

Triangle

Square

Rectangle

Circle

Triangle

Square

Parallelogram

Trapezium

Pentagon

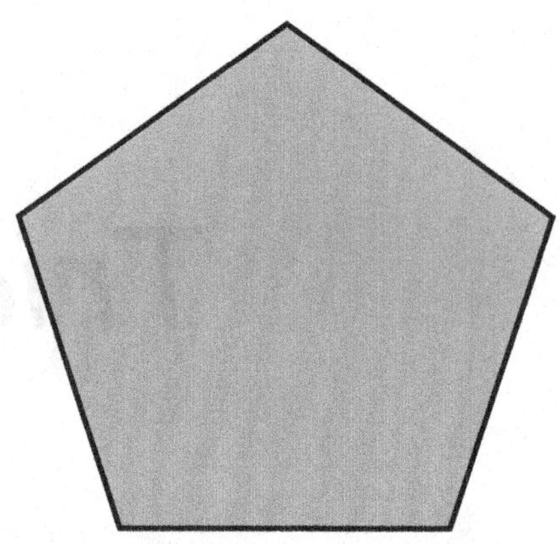

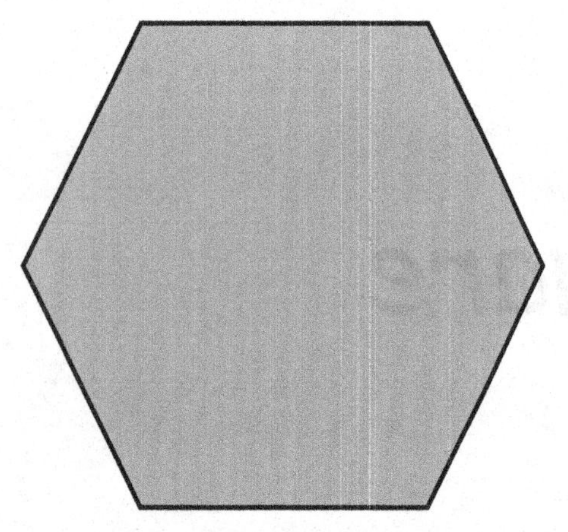

Hexagon

Parallelogram

Trapezium

Pentagon

Hexagon

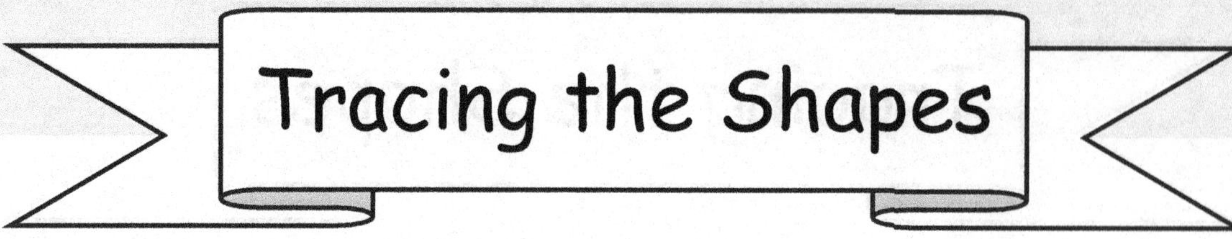

Parallelogram

Trapezium

Pentagon

Hexagon

Parallelogram

Trapezium

Pentagon

Hexagon

Ellipse

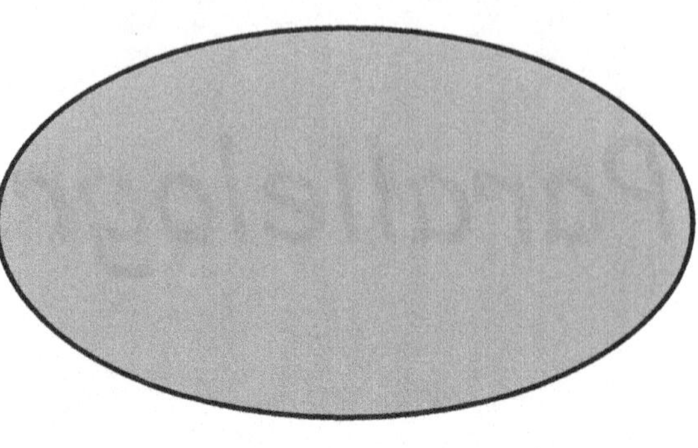

Diamond

Star

Heart

Ellipse

Diamond

Star

Heart

Ellipse

Diamond

Star

Heart

Ellipse

Diamond

Star

Heart

Identifying Shapes

Color the shapes that match the shape on the right hand.

Identifying Shapes

Color the shapes that match the picture on the left.

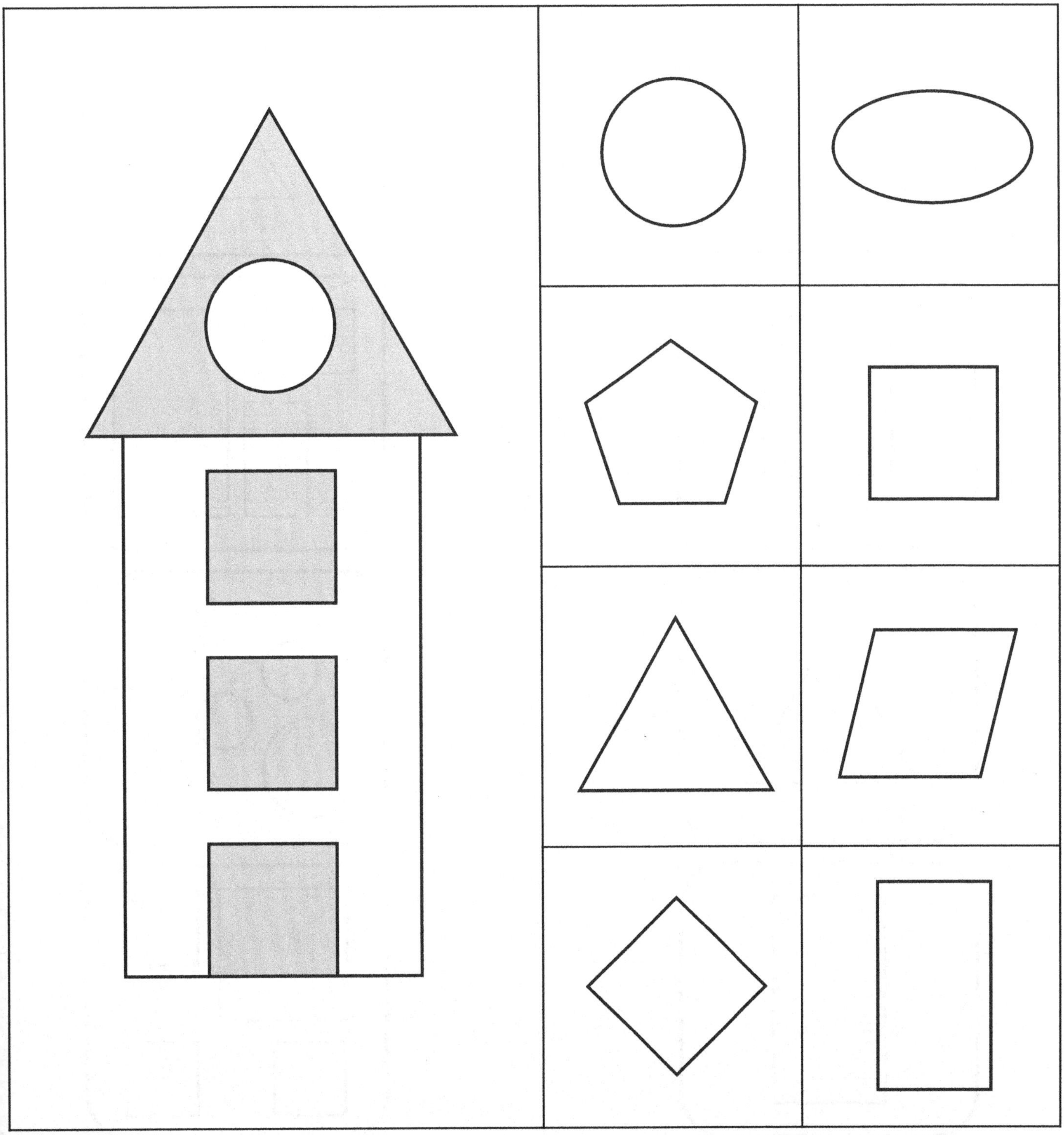

Grouping Shapes

Connect each group to the same shape.

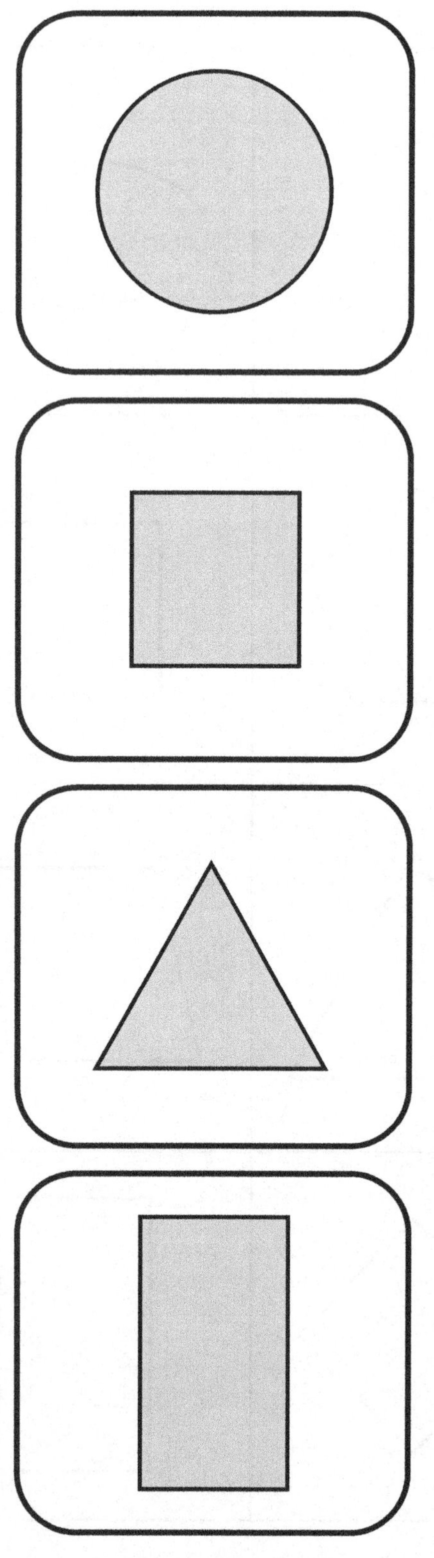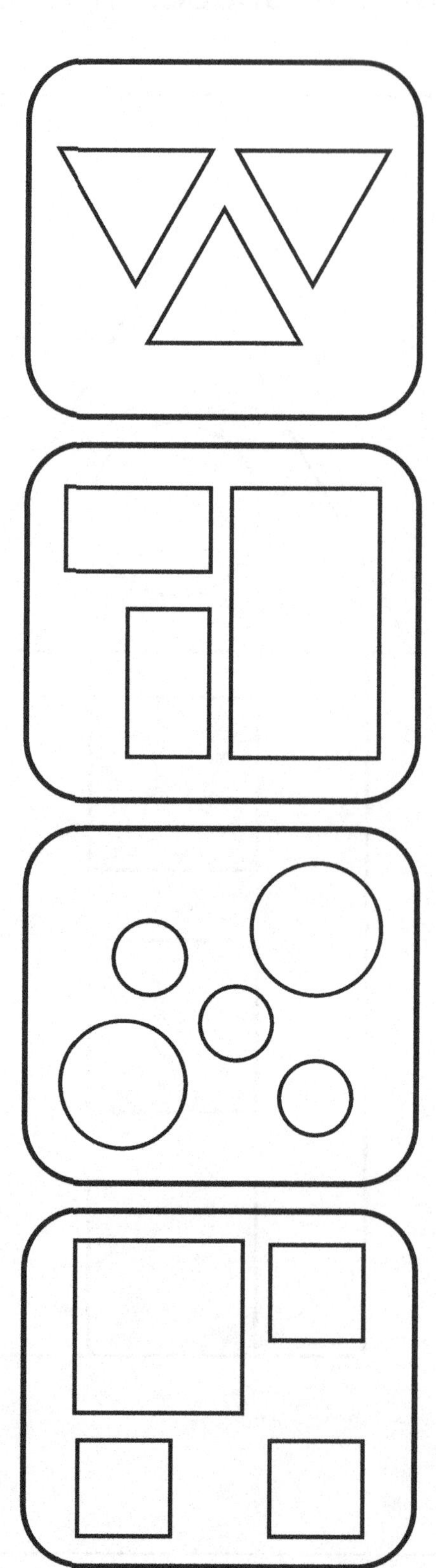

Identifying Shapes

Color the pictures by shapes.

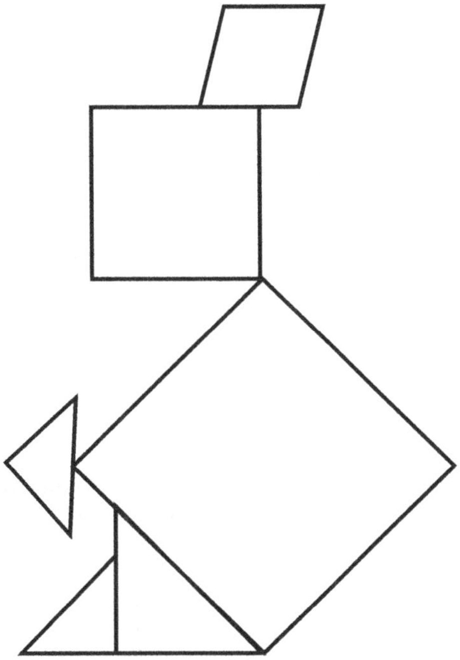

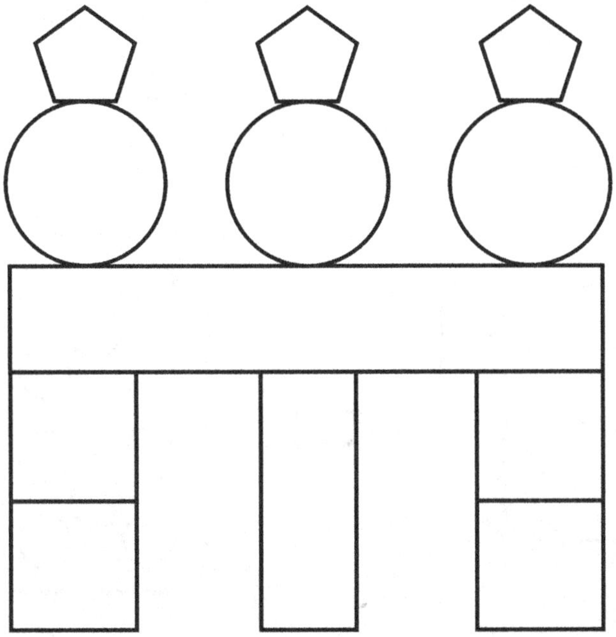

red	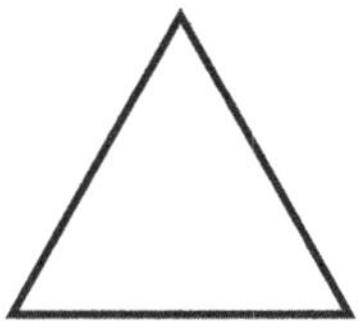 green
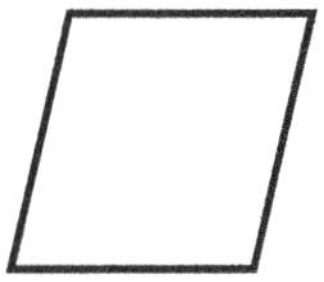 purple	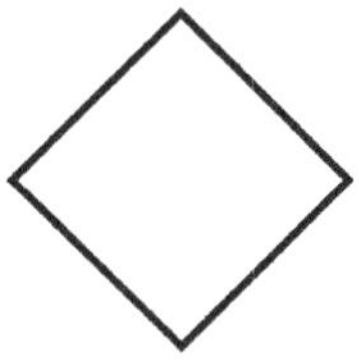 pink
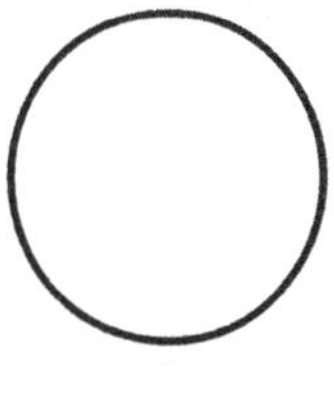 yellow	orange
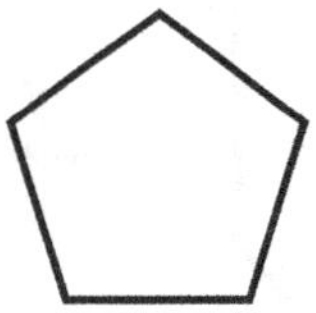 blue	 brown

Addition 0-10

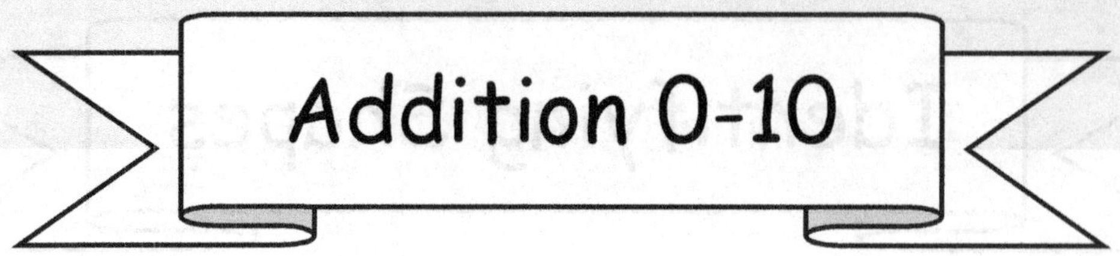

Add the dots on the cubes and color the answer in the box.

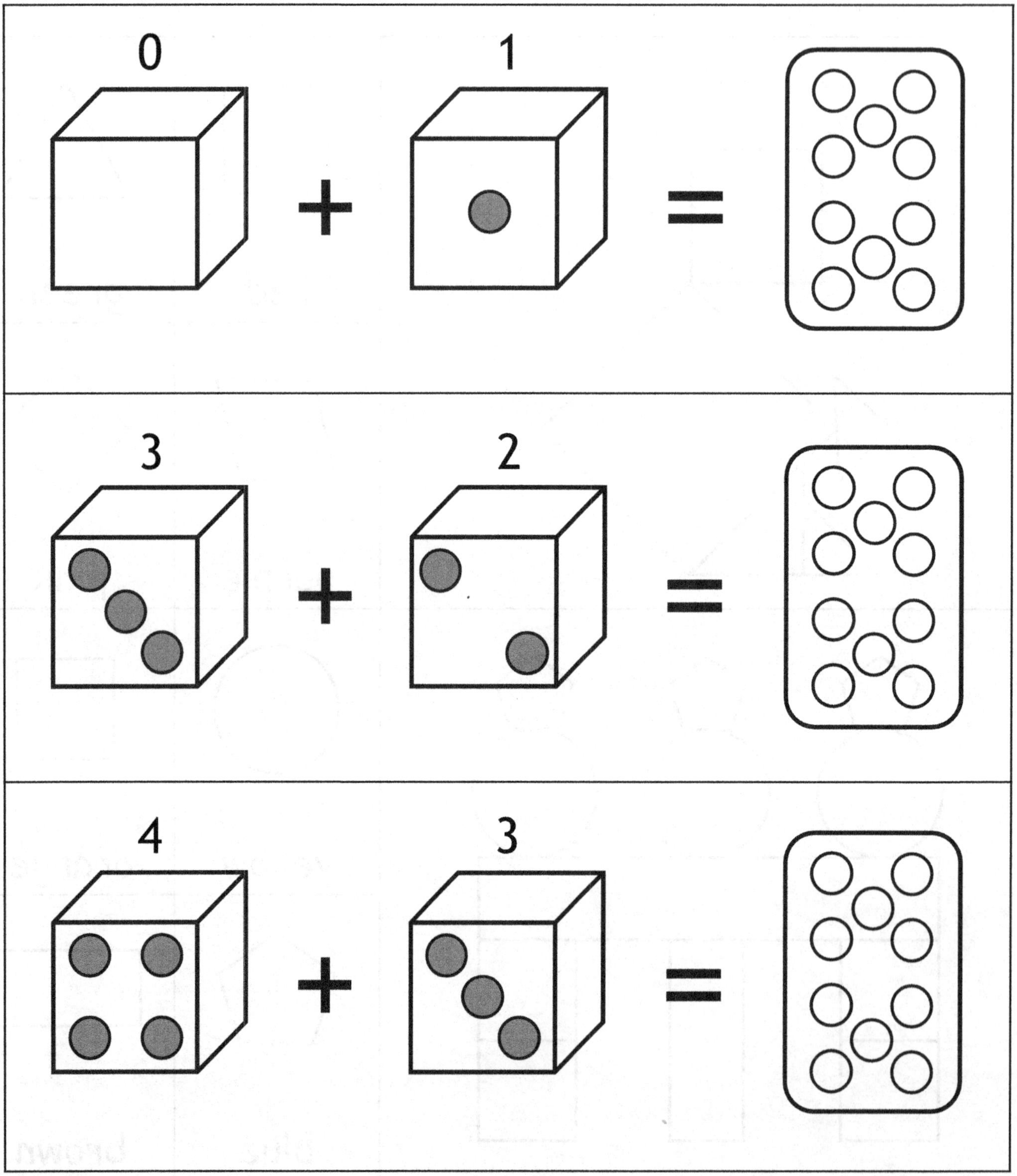

Add the dots on the cubes and color the answer in the box.

1 + 5 =

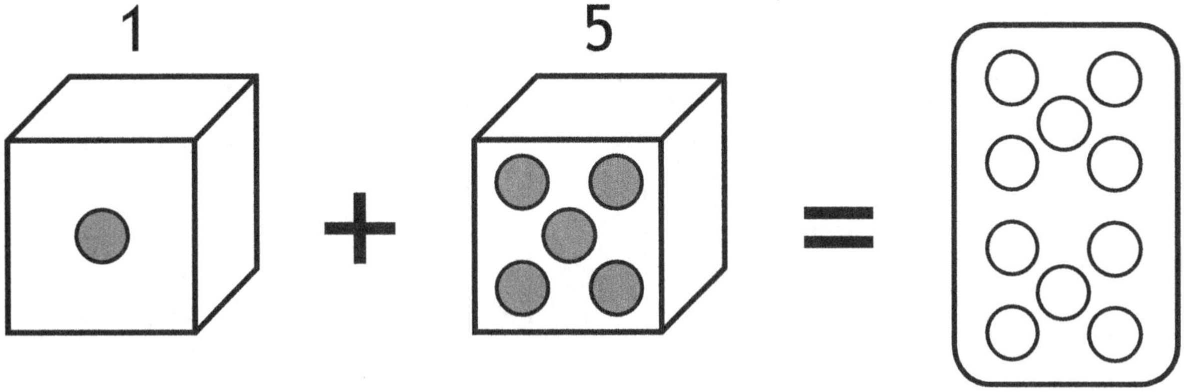

1 + 1 =

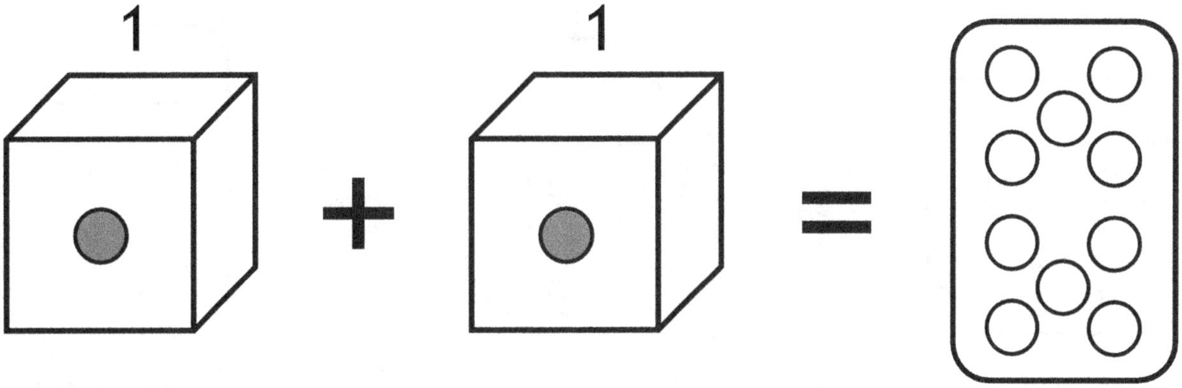

5 + 3 =

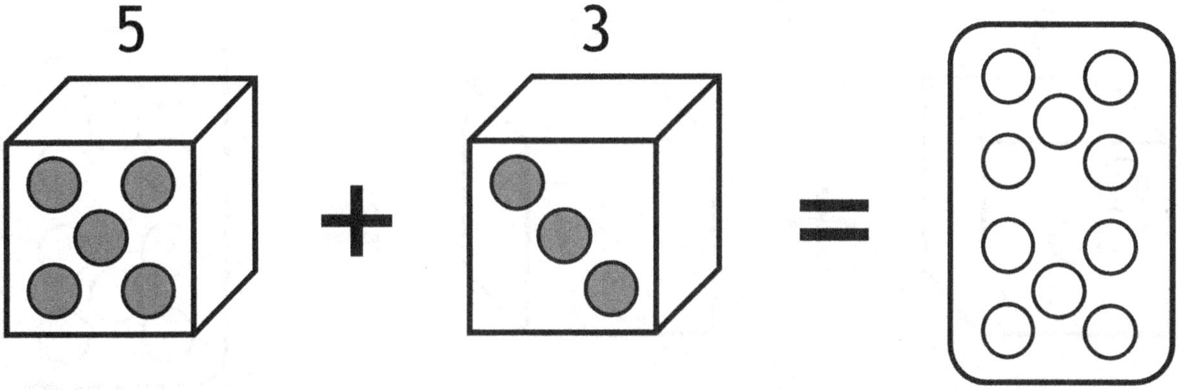

Add the dots on the cubes and color the answer in the box.

1	+	3	=	
5	+	4	=	
3	+	0	=	

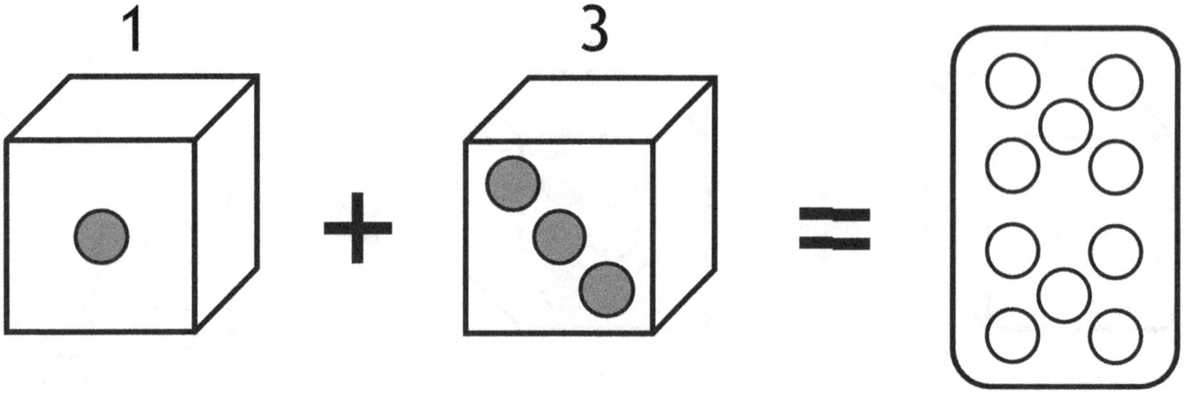

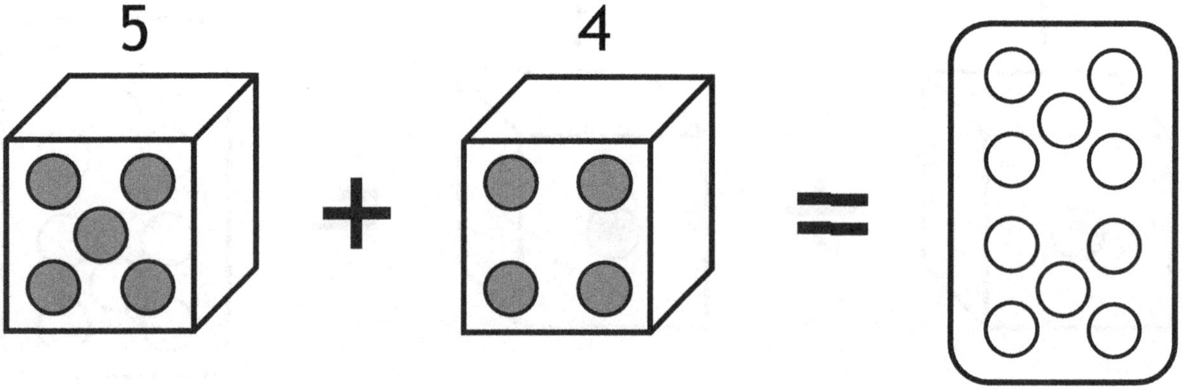

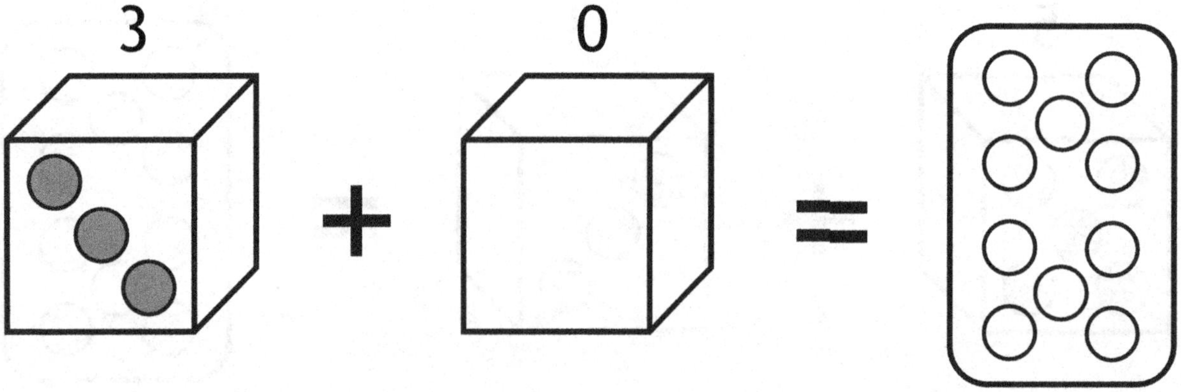

Color the ten frames, add and write the answer in the box.

7 + 1 =

3 + 7 =

5 + 3 =

Addition 0-10

Color the ten frames, add and write the answer in the box.

9 + 1 =

8 + 2 =

7 + 3 =

Addition 0-10

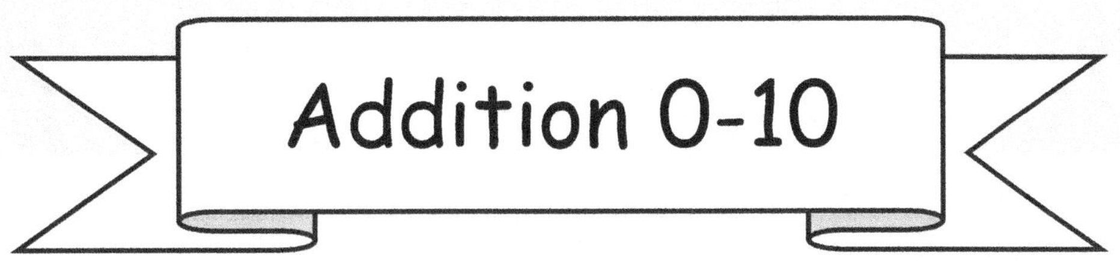

Write the number and draw the balls in the boxes to match the answer in the roof.

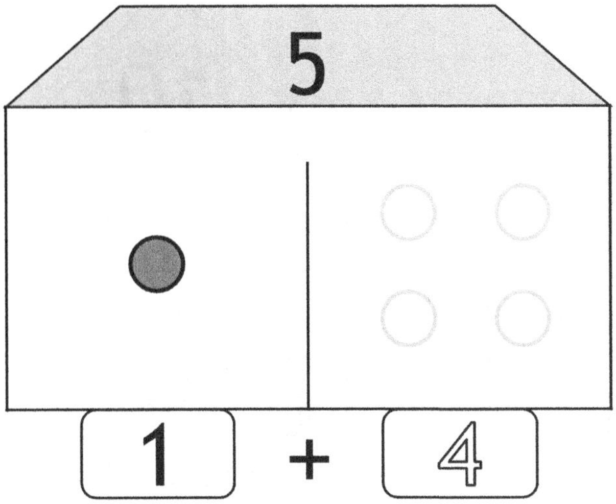

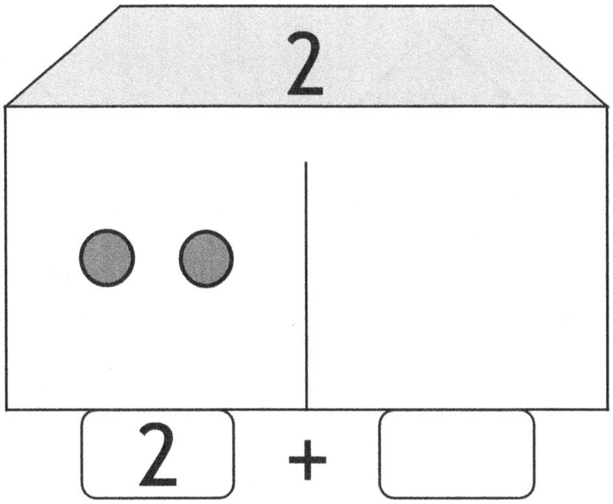

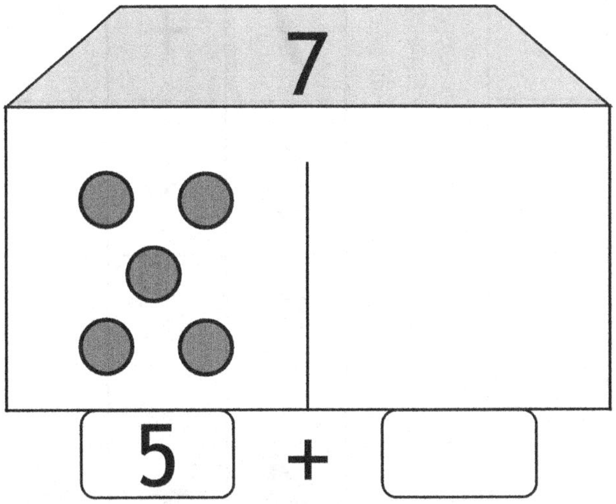

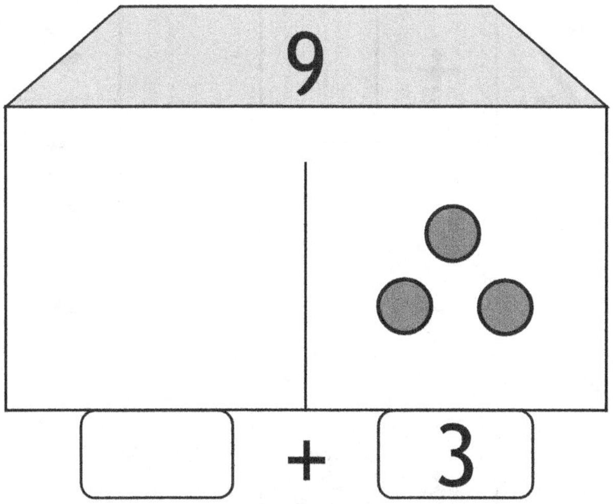

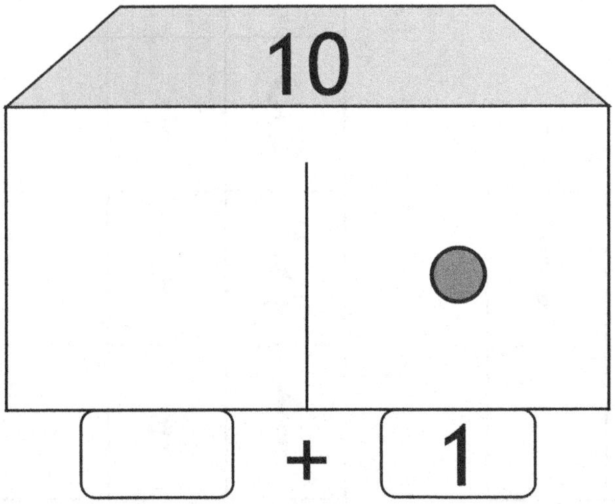

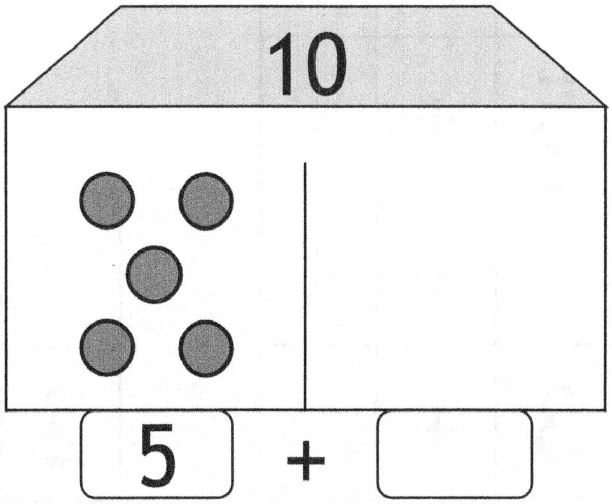

Addition 0-10

Add and write the number each floor to match the answer in the roof.

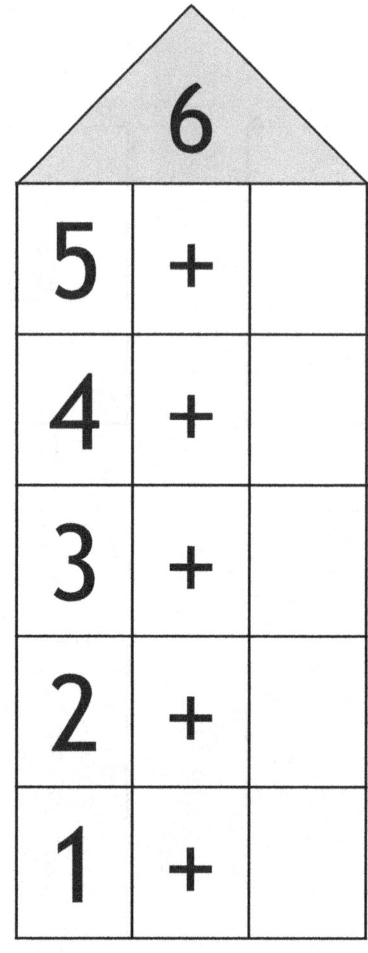

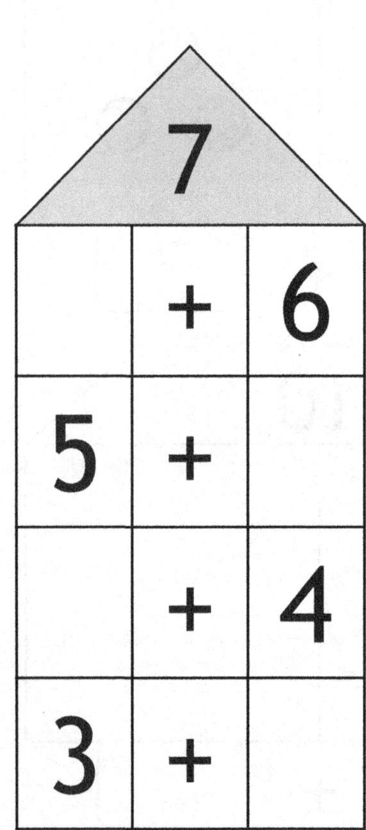

Draw, add and write the answer in the box.

Tom	Jim	Ten Frame

Tom has 2 stars and Jim has 3 stars.
How many stars do they have altogether?

[ ] + 3 = [ ]

Draw, add and write the answer in the box.

Jane has 6 birds and Lilly has 1 bird. How many birds do they have altogether?		
Jane	Lilly	Ten Frame

6 + ☐ = ☐

Draw, add and write the answer in the box.

There are 5 red balls and 4 blue balls in a box. How many balls are in the box?

Red Balls	Blue balls	Ten Frame

$$5 \quad + \quad 4 \quad =$$

Draw, add and write the answer in the box.

There are 3 girls and 3 boys in a room. How many children are in the room?		
Girls	Boys	Ten Frame

☐ + ☐ = ☐

Subtract the numbers and color the answer in the box.

3 - 2 =

6 - 3 =

10 - 1 =

Subtract the numbers and color the answer in the box.

5 - 1 =

8 - 6 =

9 - 4 =

Subtraction 0-10

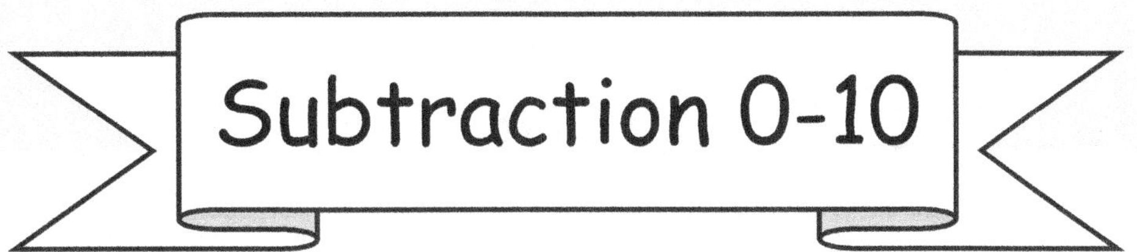

Subtract the numbers and color the answer in the box.

10 - 4 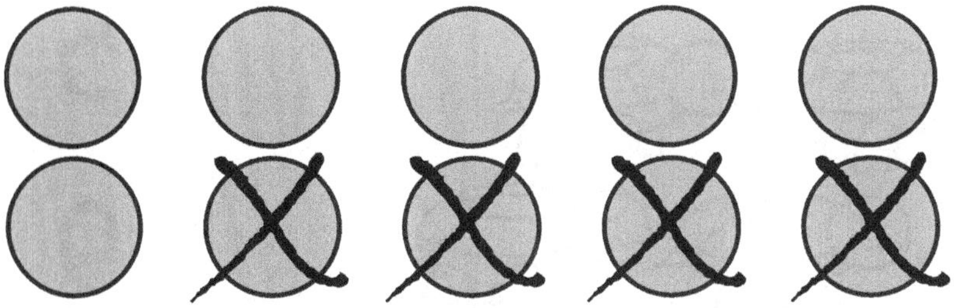	= 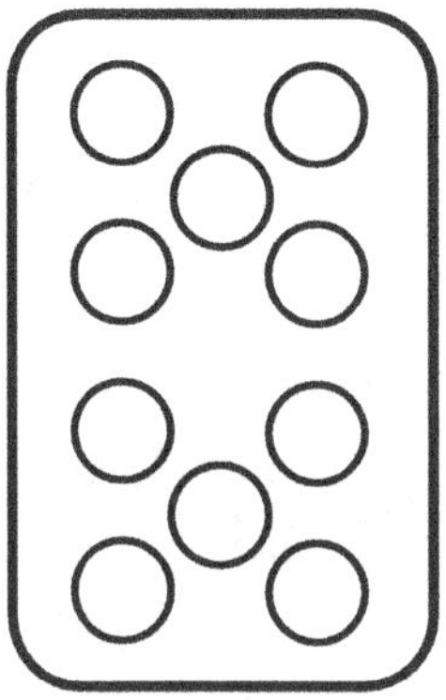
8 - 1 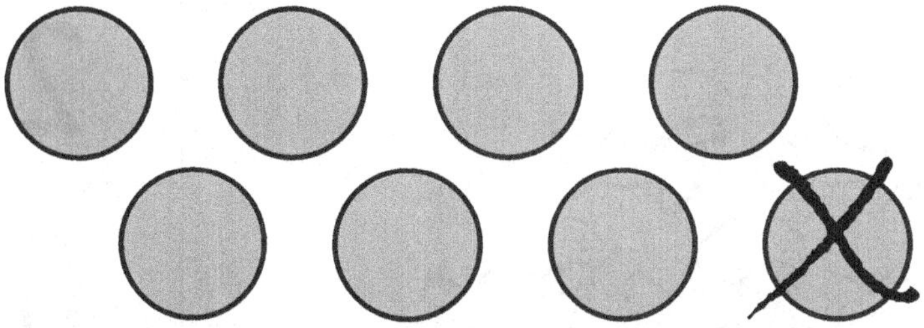	= 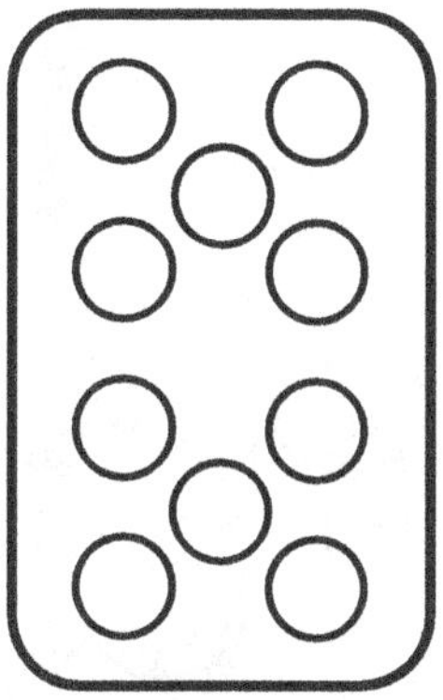
9 - 8 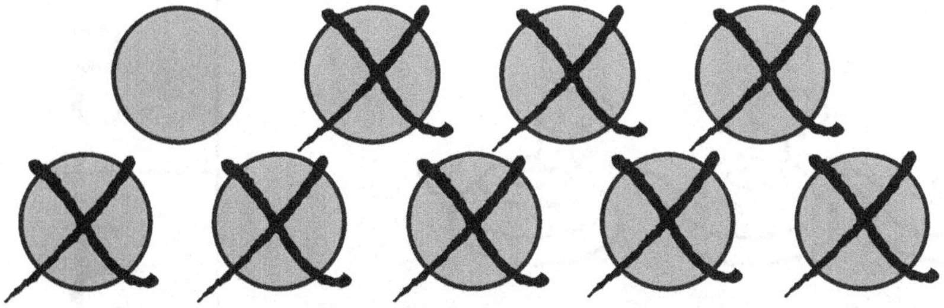	= 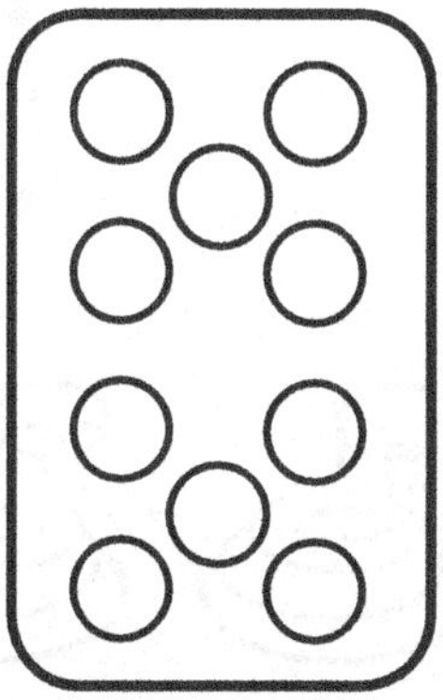

Cross out the objects and circle the right answer.

8 - 3 =

2

5

9

10 - 6 =

4

2

0

5 - 2 =

7

5

3

Cross out the objects and circle the right answer.

7 - 1	=	2
		4
		6
3 - 3	=	0
		1
		2
9 - 8	=	1
		2
		3

Subtraction 0-10

Cross out the objects to match the missing numbers.

10 - ☐ = 9

7 - ☐ = 2

4 - ☐ = 0

Cross out the objects to match the missing numbers.

6 - ☐	= 4
9 - ☐	= 5
2 - ☐	= 1

Draw, subtract and write the answer in the box.

A shop had 10 books. 5 of them were sold. How many books does the shop still have?	
Books	Ten Frame

10 - ☐ = ☐

Draw, subtract and write the answer in the box.

There were 8 penguins on the bus. 4 got off. How many penguins are still on the bus?	
Penguins	Ten Frame

$$\boxed{} - 4 = \boxed{}$$

Draw, subtract and write the answer in the box.

Pizza	Ten Frame

You had 9 slices of pizza. You ate 3 of them. How many slices of pizza do you have left?

$$9 - 3 =$$

Draw, subtract and write the answer in the box.

Balls	Ten Frame
There were 7 balls. 4 are red and the rest are green. How many balls are green?	

Follow me for more books and
        download free printable worksheets!

Website:
        https://kidzidi.com/

Facebook:
        https://www.facebook.com/apandthebooks

Twitter:
        https://twitter.com/APandtheBooks

Instagram:
        https://www.instagram.com/apandthebooks/

Pinterest:
        https://www.pinterest.com/prechavut/

Made in the USA
Monee, IL
07 July 2026